Simply Salsa

Dancing without Fear at God's Fiesta

Janet Perez Eckles

Foreword by Kathi Macias

JUDSON PRESS
PUBLISHERS SINCE 1824
VALLEY FORGE, PA

Simply Salsa: Dancing without Fear at God's Fiesta

Judson Press has made every effort to trace the ownership of all quotes. In the event of a question arising from the use of a quote, we regret any error made and will be pleased to make the necessary correction in future printings and editions of this book.

Unless otherwise indicated, Bible quotations in this volume are from THE HOLY BIBLE, NEW INTERNATIONAL VERSION®, NIV® Copyright © 1973, 1978, 1984, 2010 by Biblica, Inc.™ Used by permission. All rights reserved worldwide.

Scripture quotations marked THE MESSAGE are from *The Message*. Copyright © 1993, 1994, 1995, 1996, 2000, 2001, 2002. Used by permission of NavPress Publishing Group

Scripture quotations marked NLT are from the Holy Bible, New Living Translation, copyright © 1996, 2004, 2007 by Tyndale House Foundation. Used by permission of Tyndale House Publishers, Inc., Carol Stream, Illinois 60188. All rights reserved.

Cover and interior design by Wendy Ronga / Hampton Design Group.

Library of Congress Cataloging-in-Publication Data
Eckles, Janet Perez. Simply salsa: dancing without fear at God's fiesta / Janet Perez Eckles; foreword by Kathi Macias.—1st ed. p. cm.
ISBN 978-0-8170-1701-9 (pbk.: alk. paper) 1. Christian women—Religious life.
I. Title. BV4527.E26 2011
248.8'43—dc22   2011010429

Printed in the U.S.A.
First Edition, 2011.

Contents

Acknowledgments

I acknowledge that this blind *chica* would be sinking in self-pity if God hadn't put before me a picture of triumph through his Son, Jesus. That portrait highlights the image of those whom I love:

My hubby, Gene, the one with whom I counsel about the next step in the ministry, who always says, "I think you should go for it." He deserves all the credit for his constant support, and also for his unconditional love in all areas during our 35 years of marriage.

"I hope you like it," my mom whispers as she places a dish of food at my desk. She prepares healthy meals while I work endless hours at my computer. With tenderness, she cheers my accomplishments and dashes around to take care of anything I might need. And in her 4'11" stature, she's a true giant in my life.

My dad, whom we call "Ito," who also lost his sight, is an example of tenacity and perseverance for me.

I count on friends who, with nothing but pure love and generosity, have volunteered to be "my eyes": Cindi Lynch, Steve Meyer, Mary Wolfram, and Jeanne Zeiser. With their help, I'm not blind anymore because they've allowed me to see the beauty of true friendship.

When the tasks are too much and the sea of challenges seems daunting, God brings me to an island of joy. There I have my son Jason, his wife Rachel, my two grandchildren, Kam and Aly, my son Jeff, and our youngest son, Joe, who is in the glory of heaven. They remind me of God's grace for the gifts they are to me. And in gratitude, my passion is refueled to continue writing with devotion and commitment.

Foreword

Salsa dancing? Are you kidding me? No music or dancing can compare for getting your heart pumping, your feet tapping, and your blood flowing. But during my childhood I got the message that I didn't have the right to enjoy anything quite so much. And so I throttled back, determined to be a "grownup" who lived sensibly, obeyed the laws of the land, and pretended I wasn't bored with such a dull life.

When I was a teenager, I even spent four months in a convent, contemplating a life devoted to Christ's church. But when I confronted my own unworthiness, even in such a sacred place, I walked out of that convent, and I did not return to church for more than ten years. After all, I reasoned, what was the point? I'd tried the responsible, quiet, respectful, religious thing and still felt like a big fat failure, so why bother? It wasn't that I stopped believing in God; I just decided there was no way to please the Lord, so I might as well enjoy myself.

It had taken me twenty-six years to begin to understand that responsible and quiet and respectful—though admirable traits—just weren't enough. They weren't enough to provide me with a joyous life, and they weren't even enough to get me into heaven. But when I decided to please myself and began to stray from my responsible, respectful roots, that rebellious life didn't make me joyous either.

If only I'd had *this* book during those breaking-out years. In *Simply Salsa,* Janet Perez Eckles offers a woman like me some inspiring ways to find hope and joy—without heartbreak and regret.

Instead, ten years after leaving the church, I realized that rebellion wasn't working out very well either. By then, my mother and two brothers had all developed a personal relationship with Jesus, but I stubbornly held out. As my personal life disintegrated around me, however, I began to wonder if maybe I should investigate what they believed after all.

I called my mom one hot afternoon in July and told her what a mess I'd made of my life. Graciously, she didn't say, "Gee, what a surprise!" Instead she told me, "You need Jesus." She said a lot of other things too (which I mostly dismissed), but I did finally agree to talk to God about how I was feeling—just to get off the phone.

A few minutes later I realized I felt dirty, so I decided to take a shower. As I stood under that warm water, trying to wash away the grimy feeling, it dawned on me that the dirt wasn't on the outside. But how do you wash away dirt from your heart?

As I stepped out of the shower, I remembered my promise to my mother and decided maybe a little talk with Jesus wasn't such a bad idea.

Throwing on some clothes, I went to my room and knelt beside my bed. As I closed my eyes, I suddenly saw myself standing in a large crowd on a dusty road. The people, some weeping, some jeering, were straining to see something. I too craned my neck in an attempt to see the object of their attention.

Then I spotted Jesus. He was carrying his cross, his face and body streaked with blood and sweat as he stumbled forward. By the time he drew even with me, I too was weeping. And then he stopped. Raising his head, Jesus looked straight into my eyes and spoke five words that forever changed my life: "I did it for you."

Those early years of being "good" flashed through my mind—including the moment when I realized I would never be good enough. In that moment, I realized that I didn't *have* to do anything—Jesus had already done it! And the gift of abundant life was mine for the taking.

Oh, if there'd been a salsa band nearby at that moment, I would have jumped to my feet and danced with all my heart! But on the rock radio station playing in the background, the DJ suddenly announced a song especially for someone "out there" who needed to hear it: "Oh Happy Day" by the Edwin Hawkins Singers. And oh, what a happy day it was! My sins were indeed washed away, as my heart sang, my spirit danced, and I knew I would never be the same.

And of course, I haven't been. Though at times during the ensuing thirty-seven years I have allowed the busyness of life, the fear of failure, the guilt of past sin, and even the pressure of wanting to please and perform to drown out the music that was birthed in my heart that day, Jesus always calls me back.

"Let's dance," he reminds me. "Remember, I did it for you."

And I smile, allowing the rhythm and beat of joyous celebration to flow through my spirit once again.

In this book, *Simply Salsa: Dancing without Fear at God's Fiesta,* Janet Eckles describes moment after moment in life—her own as well as others'—when busyness, tragedy, fear, guilt, and anxiety drown out the music that Jesus wants to play in our hearts. And again and again, Janet testifies to the power of God to transform those moments of weeping or trembling into a heart-thrilling invitation to dance.

I only wish I'd had Janet's book in my own early days of learning how to truly dance through life with my hand in Jesus' hand. But at least I have it now—and I can encourage others to get it as well, not only for themselves but also for their friends. This is a lighthearted and yet profound book that speaks to women at every level—whether wallowing in the mire of self-pity, slogging through never-ending guilt, trying to outrun fear, or just plain missing out on the ecstasy of a dance-filled life. It doesn't have to be that way—and *Simply Salsa* was written to help you understand that.

Join us at the heavenly fiesta, will you? Nothing on earth is worth missing this dance!

—Kathi Macias
Award-winning author of 30+ books,
Including the "Extreme Devotion" novels
(New Hope Publishers)

www.KathiMacias.com
www.TheTitus2Women.com
http://kathieasywritermacias.blogspot.com

1
What Happened to Our Dreams?

In the face of adversity,
if God is first,
triumph replaces fear.

Bueno, chica, let's talk. The mariachi band playing our dreams has stopped. The music we once enjoyed has lost its rhythm. And the bad news blaring from the TV just adds to our personal troubles.

We sit on our unmade beds with a wrinkled tissue in hand and bite our lips. What went wrong? As little girls we felt destined for happy lives of significance and success. But along the way, the world brought unforeseen circumstances, pain that shook our senses, and heartaches that left us numb.

Buenas noticias. I've got good news. I have a clue about where we went wrong. We all bought tickets marked "Happiness and Success" and boarded the train. The only problem was that we disregarded God's purposes and mapped our routes according to our own wisdom, past experiences, and expectations. And with hearts exploding with anticipation, we reserved window seats, hoping that when the train stopped, sweet happiness wrapped in prosperity and peace awaited us, just like the kisses of our *abuela* when we visited her.

I used to be on that train, bouncing on the seat while it chugged along. But, with no warning or preparation, a change in the route brought my train to a screeching halt. Heavens! The stop was so abrupt and violent it threw me out the window. And there I was—

broken, lost, confused, and sinking into a puddle of self-pity. Physical blindness, infidelity, the murder of my child, and the acquittal of his killer—all these tragedies piled on one another in my own personal train wreck.

Dios mio! I cried to God, wondering if the Lord heard me, questioning the Spirit's presence. And that's when fear settled in. No more celebration of life, no more joy, no more fiestas with friends and family. Fear took over.

I didn't deserve this. I felt life had failed me miserably, and that stunk. I'd always been a good person, obeyed rules, took the dog to the vet, and even returned library books on time. *Que pasó?* What happened?

Perhaps you've asked yourself that same question. Whether you are Hispanic like me or not, I bet you've experienced "her-panic"! We all panic at one time or another when our life ends up in a mess. Cross-eyed with confusion and fear of tomorrow, we feel our dreams melting like *helados de chocolate* in July. And I have the feeling that our primary problem has nothing to do with extra pounds, lack of money, some big disappointment, or any other circumstance.

Amiga, it's time to figure this out. Grab your cup of *cafe con leche,* and let's talk about those times when we've ended up on the train track of disappointment while fear jeered at us. I know you've been there; we all have. And although my scars of hardship are visible if you look closely, I found the secret, the spot of hope, the security and safety we all long for...but not in the notions we grew up with. I found it in God's Word, the Holy Bible. With simplicity that soothes the soul, God reveals the solutions, not by changing our situations but by transforming our hearts.

Muchacha, for now, turn down that salsa tune, hold onto your *sombrero,* and settle into that overstuffed chair. We're about to find out what to do with broken plans and melted dreams. No matter where you are, even if your world is jammed with trials, God promises to reveal the secret to success, to lives of purpose, contentment, and confidence. God will show us how to move from a fear-filled life to a life that is faith-full.

Not Just Sweet Things

My lesson began when I left Bolivia and landed in the United States. When I was 12 years old, my mother, my 11-year-old brother, and I stood outside our La Paz home beside an old taxicab. With wrinkled fingers, my *abuela* gripped her white handkerchief and sobbed to *mami*. "Will you write as soon as you get there?"

Mami nodded, and tears shone in her eyes, too. With frail arms, my *abuela* hugged me tight, and her tears mingled with mine. I inhaled her stale perfume as she pecked my cheeks with kisses.

My heart ached at the separation from my *abuela*, the grandmother who used to soothe me with her stories and her readings from *Aesop's Fables*. I thought about how, with rosary in hand, she would call us to kneel and pray with her. Her words were always gentle, and her love was like the soft, warm afternoon breeze of La Paz. And now we had to leave her behind—and for what? To head to the United States of America, the country where people say all our dreams will come true. That's why Papi had worked for four years to gather the pile of documents the U.S. demanded. That's why he'd endured many months of separation from us. It was all so he could go and prepare a home for us in this new land.

My brother and I sat on either side of our mami on the torn back seat of the taxi. I gazed out the window at the neighborhood playground, where weeds grew among spots of rocks and dirt. The worn swing swayed back and forth as if to wave goodbye to me, and the metal slide—slick down the center, with rusty spots along the sides—blinked dully at me in the afternoon sunlight. The playground's shabby condition testified to both its constant use and lack of care. But this was my home, my neighborhood—familiar and comfortable.

The houses and dirty narrow streets of my childhood disappeared as the cab turned the corner heading to the La Paz airport. With the back of my hand, I wiped away tears while Mami patted my arm and assured me, "You're going to really like our new home."

Once we boarded the plane and took off, the small aircraft shook and dipped, making my brother sick at his stomach. I sat beside him, stuffing down a mixture of angst, fear, and apprehension.

The plane landed at a huge airport in Miami, a name that seemed funny to us at the time. We dragged our suitcases to the counter to be searched. A tall, fair-skinned man, the tallest I'd ever seen, pulled our clothes from our suitcases. With a stern look in his eye, he grabbed a plastic bag of *chuño*, held it up in the air, and then turned it and examined its contents. Wrinkling his nose, he tossed it in the trash. He did the same with the spices Mami had tucked in the corner of her bag. These were the first of a myriad of items we had to discard from the lives we knew.

Now, four decades later I understand why God pulled me from the familiar and the comfortable. The Lord had plans for me. But *caramba!* The journey hasn't all been easy. For reasons I don't know, along with the many sweet moments, God's plan mingled in some episodes that seared.

Has the Lord ever done the same to you? Have you ever been yanked from familiar, comfortable circumstances you never wanted to let go of? There you are, confused because you never imagined this turn of events. Why would God allow such ugliness to touch your life? How can a loving and good God plan that for you? These are essential questions for women of faith today, just as they were for women in biblical times.

But There's a Reason

Ruth knew what it was like to face circumstances very different from what she'd hoped and planned. Remember Ruth? She was the *señora* who was suddenly left with no *esposo*. No doubt she knew grief. She must have felt lonely and maybe fearful of the future. But she did something most of us probably wouldn't have considered. I know I never would. Of all people, she clung to Naomi, her mother-in-law. Ruth insisted on following Naomi back to her homeland, a foreign place to her.

Que? What? That's an odd decision. Why would Ruth want to hang on to the mother of her dead husband? But God was working in her heart. God placed in her a desire to change the scenery, to head to a place where things weren't familiar.

But the path wasn't easy. Obstacles got in the way. Naomi didn't want to take her with her. Naomi asks, "Am I going to have any more sons, who could become your husbands?" (Ruth 1:11). Stay here and get a life, was probably her attitude. But something was burning in Ruth's heart that compelled her to stay with Naomi. I can imagine Ruth clutching at Naomi's sleeve as she declared: "Don't urge me to leave you or to turn back from you. Where you go I will go, and where you stay I will stay. Your people will be my people and your God my God" (Ruth 1:16).

God is wonderful that way. The Lord uses the circumstances of our lives—sometimes circumstances that are not so pretty—to fulfill specific plans, amazingly wonderful plans. For Ruth, it all started when God placed a hunger in her heart for something big. And that same sort of hunger rumbles in the deepest and most intimate place in our hearts, too. It pulsates with life at every turn; it calls us with relentless insistence. It begs to be recognized, embraced, fed, nourished, and fulfilled. Ruth had it. You have it, and I do, too. Actually, there's no one on this earth who doesn't have that longing.

What we desire is "purpose"—the kind of purpose that gives breathing to our souls, life to our days, and meaning to our steps. We long to discover the very purpose for which God created us. But what is it?

Buenas noticias. Good news. We don't have to look for it. No need to figure it out or even define it. God did that for us. Jesus said the purpose of life—for you and for me—is to love the Lord our God with all our heart, mind, and soul (Matthew 22:37).

Oh my, my. Did Jesus really say that? We are to love God with *todo,* our whole selves—heart, mind, and soul? What a huge task for *chicas* like us whose plates are full of chores, tasks, and demands from the *familia.* Maybe such devotion to God was possible in biblical times when they didn't have the Internet, ATM machines, great sales at the mall, or careers to overload their time. But how can we love God that much, with that intensity, that commitment, and that depth? Heavens, that task is bigger than we can handle.

And that's why you may have done what I did when confronted with that command: I accepted the "love God" part, but I subtly dismissed the "with all your heart, mind, and soul" as irrelevant or a bit antiquated.

There's a reason many of us have done that. I believe we compromised and negotiated because we're smart *muchachas.* We figured out that the only way we could obey Jesus' command was to find our own way to love God. So that's what we did.

First, we made sure we believed in God. If someone asked if we did, we'd nod our heads so emphatically that our dangling earrings would shake for a long while.

So, that first step has been taken. We believe in God. The second step is to go to church. We did that, too. We'd go, and we'd smile at those around us, and then come home with the satisfaction that we did more than most.

Next, we pray. Goodness gracious, our prayers are *importantes,* because that's how we hand the Lord a list of what we want, need, and long for. But I did more than just ask God for what I wanted—I always remembered to thank God for what I had. That took care of any guilt that might creep up.

And, finally, we try—really *try*—to be good people.

So there you have it. We found a way to love God that would fit into our schedule. And maybe we've even convinced ourselves that it works for us.

How Did We Do That?

Right about now, dip your tortilla in some guacamole and take a bite, because you'll need energy to swallow this truth: If we don't love God with all our heart, mind, and soul, we'll end up loving other stuff or people or dreams or aspirations or goals much more than we should.

Think I'm kidding? I know this truth from experience. This *chica* ended up loving her life more than God. I'm talking honestly here. I wanted my life to be painless, successful, prosperous, happy, pleasant, and peaceful. So I fell in love with the plans that would take me to those goals. I loved God, too—because I needed the Lord to make sure those plans worked out. I needed God's assistance in making my dreams become reality. Yes, I did.

Amigas, heat is surging from my chest to my head because I'm about to spill more gritty details. I started out by holding my head high because I was diligent in following the world's directives: Follow your dreams, don't let anyone stop you, craft your own plan for your life, live to the fullest, and enjoy life. What a logical approach, right? It was tasty and alluring, like my *abuela's* honey-glazed *buñuelos*. So I took a large bite of that "follow your dreams" pastry. Indigestion didn't come on right away because I made fulfilling those dreams my purpose in life, and I pursued it with great passion.

For many years, my efforts seemed to be paying off. I graduated from college with honors, and then found *mi esposo*, a man who fit the criteria I'd listed in my teen years. I gave birth to three great kids—all healthy and smart. I went on a diet and exercised to recover my pre-pregnancy figure, and made sure I was the kind of wife who encouraged hubby to climb the corporate ladder, supporting him all the way up. Life smiled at me. We built a beautiful two-story home. I was doing what I wanted to do—staying home to care for my three sons. We enjoyed the amenities of suburban America and drove BMWs.

My life looked delicious, but deep inside me there was a hunger for complete satisfaction and peace. Nonetheless, I forged on, trying to quiet that "there's got to be more" nagging. I bought more, decorated better, improved, fixed, and enhanced every area of my life the best I could. And day after day, I danced a complicated *salsa* to keep up with my daily desires.

A Bit Desperate

Then, with no warning, like the sudden cold wind from the Andes Mountains, a shocking, icy gust chilled my world.

"I can see a definite decrease in your field of vision," the ophthalmologist said. "There's *nada*, nothing, anyone can do. You need to be prepared."

I tried to ignore the queasiness in my stomach. I knew I had a hereditary retinal disease, but the doctors had told me it wouldn't affect my vision until age sixty. I was only thirty-one, and my sons were three, five, and seven. That wasn't fair. The doctors had lied to me.

But being the determined *chica* that I was, I stayed focused on my dreams. I kept on dancing to keep up the image of success. Yet from time to time, the thought of losing my sight made me stop in my tracks. And that's when I muttered sincere but desperate prayers—sometimes in English, sometimes in Spanglish.

Months swept by, and my nights became longer. I couldn't sleep because my mind kept replaying episodes of that day when I'd run into furniture, into the kids, into open doors. I was losing more and more sight. Desperate, I dashed to anyone who offered even a ray of hope for me. But all the doctors, specialists, acupuncturists, and herbalists simply increased my frustration while decreasing the balance in our bank account.

Then, about eighteen months later, the day came when I awoke and, to my horror, I saw nothing. My world had turned black.

I shook my fist at God. *Por qué?* Why me? I didn't deserve blindness. I had begged for a miracle, and God had denied me. Anger, bitterness, and fear accompanied me as I groped through the house trying to care for my small sons.

There went my dreams, sliding down the tunnel of despair. My plans, longings, and desires vanished into a world that had become a dark prison with no hope of getting out. Fear of the unknown tormented me. How would I be able to live as a blind person? What would happen to my kids? What will my husband do with a blind wife? What purpose would my life serve? Those fears gnawed at me because the plan I'd made for myself didn't include this episode. I'd always been a good person. I felt I was being punished for something I hadn't done.

Then a drastic change came about. A friend invited me to her church, and I started attending with her. Often I would sit there cradling my pain, tears rolling down my face, and my heart exploding with terror. But then one day, during the church service, a Bible verse sizzled my heart, like water hitting a hot frying pan. It was Matthew 6:33, which says to seek God and God's righteousness first, and all our needs would be met.

There it was, a brilliant light of truth, of revelation and of freedom, shining through the darkness in my life. I had made the desperate search for a cure for my eyesight my number one priority, because without the ability to see, my purpose for life, as I had defined it, was gone. I had no goals, no passion, no hope, no joy; just broken dreams and failed plans. I was one sorry *chica*.

But God whispered, "Seek me first, love me first, long for me first, and fill your heart with me first; then you'll see what I have in store for you." That's how I heard God's promise to me. And that soft calling turned the key that would unlock my musty prison.

I dried my tears, gave a long sigh, and hopped in the back seat of the divine taxicab. As we drove away, I looked back through the window at the dirty playground where I'd once entertained my shallow dreams. I reviewed for the last time the rusty slide where my passion and my purpose had enjoyed the thrill of the moment. I took one last look at rock and weeds that were scattered around the life I was leaving behind.

With expectation before me, I arrived at the airport of God's grace. The dreams I'd packed earlier were tossed away. I replaced them with a healthier desire to learn how to love God with all my heart, mind, and soul. That's right—I said, "learn," because just as I'd had to learn a new language and culture, I had to learn how to love the Lord...his way. Not halfway. Not my way. Not by doing what seemed most convenient or taking the shortcuts. I had to learn to love God with all my heart, mind, and soul.

It began in each morning as I directed my thoughts to the Lord, pondering on the Spirit's sweet way of providing what I needed for that day. Then it followed by thanking God for the good things. Even if I had no eyesight, I still had ears to hear, legs to walk, a heart to love, a family to care for, and a future crafted by God's own hands.

A New Revelation

I found that when we choose to love the Lord, it sparks a hunger to peek into God's characteristics: the unending compassion God has when we mess up; God's immense patience during the years we chase our own plans; God's stern words when admonishing against something that will cause us pain. And here's a new revelation that entered my previously confused head: Loving God means spending time soaking up God's Word. It means drinking in the promises of God's comfort when the world slaps our senses, when others reject us, and when pain comes even from those we love.

To love God is to trust when the Scripture says that if we invite the Son, Jesus, to be our Savior, we conquer death. To truly love God is to believe we can live abundantly, no matter what diagnosis, threat, or evil hovers about.

Amiga, maybe your situation isn't as drastic as mine. Or maybe it's even more painful. Life brings all kinds of ugly stuff. But the real *problema* is not our circumstances; it's how we respond. We must make the choice to leave the rusty swing set and the worn slide behind and move to a better land where God's purpose shines through the darkness and confusion.

That's what Ruth did. She was willing to travel to a new land, one that was unfamiliar but more promising. She wanted to follow God more than anything else. More than her comfort. More than her familiar home. More than her pride. And more than her own desires and hopes.

Bumps came into Ruth's life, and sometimes things were difficult as she followed through with her commitment. But God saw her heart, inhaled the sweet scent of her obedience, delighted in her trust, smiled at her humility, and sighed with pleasure at her grateful heart. The Lord revealed a solution for her dilemma that led to her becoming nothing less than a link in our Savior's lineage.

"Love God with all your heart, mind, and soul." This is the greatest commandment, the first, and the most important. And it's also the one God has put in place for our protection. *Sí*, this commandment is to protect us from confusion and fear. When we decide to love the way God commands, life becomes clearer. Whereas we once were blinded by storms, now we can see. We can gaze at God's healing rather than sink in sorrow. We can watch the trace of God's hand instead of succumbing to anxiety. And we can place our trust in the God who says, "I will rescue those who love me, I will protect those who trust in my name" (Psalm 91:14, NLT).

Initially, I viewed my blindness with shock. But God opened my spiritual eyes, rescued me, and scooped me up from the emptiness that surrounded me. And rather than feeling bitterness in my heart, I crossed the bridge from the blindness of my soul to the clarity of God's ways.

And Then God Smiles

Bueno, amiga. It's time for you to close your own eyes. Lean back and think—really think. What circumstance in your life is God using to whisper to you? If you turn your head and listen, the Spirit's calling might be clearer than you thought. The Lord definitely longs to guide you to a life rich with God's purpose and abundant with God's wealth—a wealth that has nothing to do with a bank account, but everything to do with peace and contentment, no matter the situation.

God smiles when we make loving with all our heart, mind, and soul the top priority in our lives. Then, when we do experience moments of loneliness, God's secure arms are enough. When sorrow filters through, God's compassion whispers more personally. When the world rejects us, God's unconditional acceptance soothes more deeply. When a devastating diagnosis shakes us to our very foundation, God's promises resound more sweetly. When hopelessness mocks, God's power lifts us higher.

And My Plans?

Perhaps none of this is new to you. Maybe you've heard it all before. But if you are like I was, a sliver of doubt is still poking through. And curiosity prompts the logical question. You sag your shoulders and ask, "What about *my own plans?*"

"For I know the plans I have for you," says the Lord back to you, "plans to prosper you and not to harm you, plans to give you hope and a future" (Jeremiah 29:11). Those plans are for you, for me, and for every *chica* who decides to dump the senseless notion that prosperity, hope, and a better future come from this world. We must scrap those misconceptions about what will give us significance and fulfillment. And with the same strength we use to remove the cheese stuck at the bottom of the tamale casserole, we must scrape away the "loves" that give us a false sense of purpose and satisfaction.

Now there's room for the love for *Dios*. That's when the music begins. The Lord guides you to the dance floor of your new life, sweet with purpose, significance, and grace. *Amiga*, the change in you will be so delightfully drastic that friends and family will take a second look at your radiant face and, with eyes the size of tortillas, will point at you and ask, "What happened to her?"

2

What's Wrong with *La Vida Loca*?

Holding on to a dark past carries fear into the future.

I know, *amiga*, you're about to complain, "Love God with all my heart, mind, and soul? How do you expect me to do that? You don't know the life I live, the pain that throbs night and day, or the ugly past I've had?"

I say *bienvenida*—welcome to the club. All of us can peek at our hearts and get nauseated if we stare too long at the yuck from the past. And sometimes it can be tough to leave it behind. The consequences of the past often show up in the *vida loca* some of us slide into. Maybe you know some of these women.

For example, here's a woman who stands waiting on the street corner pretty much every night, certain she'll have clients. When a man walks by, she gives a flirty smile. And with bracelets dangling from her wrist, she waves her hand. "This way to my place." Lots of necklaces hang around her neck, and her braided hair highlights her tanned complexion. But this is no twenty-first-century *chica*. I'm talking about Rahab. You know her: The prostitute who made her mark in Scripture.

So what's the deal? What would have possessed her to lure those sweaty, dirty men who'd just hopped off their camels after a long trip in that hot desert? She didn't care about their looks, backgrounds, or morals. She had a job to do, and she wasn't shy about closing the tent flap to service them. Go ahead, *amiga*, gasp all you want. That's the reality of those who choose to engage in *la vida loca*. That crazy life was probably a bit attractive to Rahab at first. The pay was better than other jobs, and the work wasn't hard. But the wear and tear on her soul and heart must have pained her every night. Her sleep was probably restless, and her dreams just a blur in the desert sand.

I believe there was a voice inside Rahab that kept saying, "No, I will not go down this road. I deserve better. I am worthy of more." But she refused to listen to that voice. Instead, she continued to humiliate herself before strange men who tore at her self-image.

Rahab was suffering from the UP syndrome, an ailment that shapes the lives of so many women, then and now. I know, you've never heard of it. I hadn't either. I'll tell you what it means in a moment. But first, hang on with me and listen to the story of another *chica* living *la vida loca*. Although she wasn't sucked into the same profession as Rahab, she lived for the easy, fun, and exciting life.

I Just Want to Dance

"I'm leaving," Maribel called out, as the door closed behind her. It was about 10:00 p.m. She was wearing pantyhose that were the perfect color to compliment her short skirt, which showed more leg than you'd see in a whole bucket of Kentucky Fried Chicken. She figured she'd earned the right to stay out half the night after her kids were in bed. And her husband didn't take his eyes from the TV, as her high heels clicked across the tile floor and out the door.

She was married and had two kids, yet her heart longed for spicy music, men who flattered her, and the buzz from dangerous drugs. She seemed to have an unquenchable desire to dance night after night. Her husband was about to leave her, but her thirst for other men lured her with a power stronger than the cocaine she used.

She was too numb to feel guilty about her choices. Her green eyes shone with an empty imitation of happiness. Her nights were loud with laughter, but her days taunted her with the silence of the dead-end life she'd carved out for herself. Maribel, a sorry *chica* living a crazy life. And you guessed it: she too was a victim of the UP syndrome.

I Need the Money

Trina's circumstances resembled Maribel's. She relished the good money she received as an exotic dancer. She could make more in one night dancing than in a week working as a cashier. The men who came to see her dance disgusted her, but the thought of the benefits and the growing bank account made the experience bearable. Night after night she steeled herself to endure their stares and hideous remarks. And yes, the UP syndrome gripped her as well.

Okay, I'll throw my life in here too. During my college years, although I wasn't promiscuous, I did prefer an exciting life that included lots of attention from the guys on campus. Once I had studied for upcoming tests, I focused on the approaching weekend. Had the phone in the dorm rung yet? Back then we had only one phone to share with all the girls on the dorm floor. Whenever it rang, we all hoped it would be for us.

Pride aside, many times the call was for me. *Sí, que bueno*, that's good, another guy inviting me to go out. That took care of Friday night, but what about Saturday night and Sunday afternoon? I needed dates then, too. Being a *muchacha* who worked hard to look good, I was usually able to find a date. In fact, as my closest friends from college can testify, some nights I had two dates, one early in the evening and other later on. There was no sex, just endless flirting as I soaked in their compliments and flattering remarks that filled the insecurity burning within me. Do I dare say that my behavior was a result of the UP syndrome?

And how about my good friend Nancy? She dashed from one lively college party to another, and the drinks she sipped all night swept through her bloodstream quickly. Alone during the day, she would purge after every meal. Heavens! She feared those extra pounds would show, and the image of perfection she'd crafted would crumble. Her addiction to drinking and binge eating caused her to cry herself to sleep. Did Nancy have an UP? You bet!

Victim Lingerie

So what's going on with these young *chicas*? Don't they know better? All of them, including me, are sorry victims of the UP syndrome—the Ugly Past. It's ugly because we didn't deserve it or ask for it or know how to handle it. Just about any woman can be plagued by her past—the woman next door, a leader in our church, a coworker, an aunt, a life-long friend. We can't always see it because most of us manage to bury our UP deep—really deep.

All of us are made up of what we have experienced—including episodes of hurt, rejection, abuse, unfairness, and mistreatment. These are all patched together as part of the quilt of our adulthood. And let's spill the truth: Because of the UP, most of us are stuck with the sad habit of blowing out long sighs that end with a sorry whimper. We end up doing all out shopping in a store called "Victoria's Victims." But did you know that wearing the "victim" lingerie is incredibly unflattering? It's really distasteful. But before I say any more about that, let's take a look at the UP of the women I've just mentioned.

Scripture doesn't reveal much about Rahab's past, but we know she grew up in a pagan society, one that did not love God or follow God's precepts. This is not pure, sweet Esther we're talking about here. Rahab's childhood may well have been like many others who live the crazy life—marred with wounds, pain, and scars that still sting.

While we don't know much about Rahab's history, we do know the reason behind Maribel's thirst to live the crazy *vida*. While she was growing up, her apartment housed a place of occult worship. Maribel's father was sure to follow each bizarre and evil ritual, which included animal sacrifices and the offering of fruit, flowers, and feathers to please the various gods and saints. Henry, the closest friend of Maribel's father, led the practice of these scary rituals, spending a great deal of time in her family's apartment. One day, Henry gave her a sardonic smile and pulled her close. His warm, smelly breath made her shudder as he told her, "You know you're ugly and you'll always be a nobody."

Maribel's father visited mediums, performed mysterious rituals, and forced her mother to perform them, too. At her father's demand, Maribel's mother would bathe the young girl in a tub filled with gardenias and strong perfumes bought at the neighborhood *botanica*. He believed these special baths would ward off bad spirits. As a teen, Maribel stayed in her room, trying to protect her younger sister from their father's physical and emotional abuse. The only way to be safe from his beatings was to pretend they agreed with his irrational accusations and obey his bizarre whims. Can you blame Maribel from trying to ease that pain?

Trina spent her painful childhood in a series of foster homes, where she felt empty and insecure. She never knew her father, and her young heart ached when she was separated from her siblings. Worse, her mother was mentally unbalanced, and during her brief supervised visits, she treated Trina cruelly.

Now let's go to my past. My situation wasn't as dramatic as Maribel's or Trina's. While still in Bolivia, my family lived with my maternal grandparents. Before I was born, my grandfather had undergone a brain treatment in an attempt to cure his alcoholism. This treatment resulted in a serious mental disorder that prompted frightful behavior. My grandfather often exploded into violent episodes of emotional and verbal abuse. As a little girl, I clung to my *mami* for protection and nurturing. But deep in my five-year-old heart, I hungered for the love and affection of my *papi*. I longed to hear him say he was proud of me. But he was struggling with his own no-win situation. Unable to earn enough money to leave my grandparents' home, *Papi* carried a great deal of grief in his heart. His frustration probably kept him from showing me any affection or affirmation. I carried that empty spot in my heart into my college days, where I sought to fill the emptiness with the attention and affection of college men.

Outwardly pretty and popular, Nancy was a vivacious cheerleader and model student. But behind her cheerleader uniform, she hid anxious insecurity—a constant fear of failing and losing others' approval, especially that of her dad, whom she adored. One day he asked, "Are you putting on some weight?" His words spoke what she feared—that she wasn't perfect anymore. Confused, she sought comfort in a full bag of cookies. Then guilt became a dangerous cycle, turning into an eating disorder and, eventually, to alcoholism.

But What about My Mess

I bet I know what you're thinking, *amiga*. You are probably saying to yourself: "Sure, these women have had some troubles, but you don't know the nightmares I've been through." And you're right. I don't know your story.

But here's what I *do* know: Every single one of us has some kind of ugly past. We all struggle with the UP syndrome. We all carry deep scars from experiences we've had as *niñas*, as young adults, or even as grown women. Yes, some of us have known disappointments the size of Brazil. And memories of those events can chisel at our hearts until they won't stop bleeding.

Here's some startling news: Pain, disappointment, sorrow, and heartache don't discriminate. They don't care about our age, our ethnicity, or whether we're well dressed or living on welfare. And the degree of the trauma we've experienced or the time it entered our life is not what's most important. What's most important is that we recognize the effects the UP has in our present life. Not only the effects of the events themselves, but the effects of our desperate attempts to hide what we've been though. We're make-up artists who have mastered the skill of covering what sears inside. We slop on spiritual make-up to mask the pain, put on foundation to conceal the tracks of our tears, and force a smile. But pretty soon, our eyes begin to show the heartache beneath that black mascara, and the strain of dragging that heavy burden makes our bones ache.

Then fear and anger add to the mess. We're so afraid we won't fit in, we won't measure up, and inadequacy becomes part of our thinking. Sometimes these thoughts are subdued. Other times they scream so loudly we can hear nothing else. But they never, ever let up. Instead, they simply grow in power because we let them. The constant wrestling causes anger to bubble up. And before we know it, we accept that we've got no choice but to live these lives of inadequacy, fear, and anger. We think it's who we were meant to be. We settle into that victim mode and shuffle through life dragging that UP everwhere we go.

Have you ever met a *chica* like that? Too many of us walk around as if there's a chain around our neck that's connected to a garbage can. We stuff all the garbage from the past into that can and drag it behind us. And pretty soon the weight tightens the chain around our neck, rubbing the skin raw. What other options do we have but to find the salve of food addictions, shopping, alcohol, drugs, or sex to ease the pain?

Taking Down the Rearview Mirror

Amigas, I'm not telling you anything new or extraordinarily revealing. This is the reality of the stuff of life. But each of us has a choice about how we'll respond. Either we carry our UP with us to the grave, or we do a wonderful thing—release it.

Caramba! How in the world do we do that? A better question might be: Do we want to do that? Digging up that past, reliving the memories, reviewing the painful details might bring up garbage we don't want to stomach right now. True. That can happen.

But maybe it's time to lift your chin, hold your shoulders back, and do what each of the friends whose stories you've just read did: Decide to leave the past in the past. And *arriba!* You can choose to live a full life now.

Life isn't meant to be conjugated like a verb—with past tense, a present tense, and a future tense. A life of significance is never lived in the past tense—only present and future. So dwelling in the past has no place for us *chicas* who have made the decision to shop at Victoria's Victory. And with Latina boldness, we can move forward, deciding never again to look in the rearview mirror of our life.

So, Where Do You Begin?

Right about now, you might want to grip me by the shoulders and shake me so hard that the curl will fall out of my hair. You want to look me in the eye and with gritted teeth you want to shout, "I can't do it. I tried to get rid of my UP, but I can't!"

If that's how you are feeling, I want to throw my fist in the air and celebrate with a loud, "Yes!" Why? Because you just took the first step. You've recognized there's nothing worthwhile—absolutely *nada*—you can do on your own. But that means you're on the

way to healing. Recognizing our frailty is the first step. Like pluck-
ing the feathers before our *abuelas* boiled the chicken, recognizing
we need help is the first step to victory.

Jesus, the divine healer, the King of kings, is the only one who has
the power to cut the chain that binds us, to set us free, and to brush
his healing fingers across the raw spot on our neck marked by the
chain we once dragged. Is it easy? No. It's tough because we've
grown used to the smell of the garbage. In fact, pitiful as it sounds,
we subtly insist it's more comfortable to keep going with what's
familiar. It's easier to continue living in the prison we've built with
bars of excuses. Excuses? Ouch! That hurts…because it's true.

And the "UP" Goes Down

But, knowing our hunger to be set free, Jesus already has his hand
outstretched toward us. And if we stand still while he draws close
enough to break that chain, we will taste a freedom that's more
delicious than *abuela's* flan. While relishing that liberation, we can
expect wonderful things to happen.

That's what happened with Rahab when she recognized who
God was. Having heard of the wonderful deeds of Israel's God, she
chose to do what was needed to save those who followed the Lord.
Don't you wish the Bible told us more about exactly how her transformation really happened? Or when she repented and how?
When she chose to turn away from the *vida loca* she'd lived, or
even when she made a different commitment? But even though
God chose not to reveal those details, we do know that she became
a woman with a sacred anointing, a special purpose, a definite
plan, and an amazing future. She became a link in the lineage of
Jesus, the Savior of humanity. Can you imagine?

So, if God gave Rahab such a divine position in spite of her background, past sin, shameful behavior, and pitiful self-worth, the

Lord will also have plans for you and me—no matter what we've done, what we endured, whatever behavior made others gasp, or even where we've been.

Maribel experienced this transformation and renewed life. When she met Jesus, she said, "No more." She repented and said, "Jesus, be my Lord and my all."

The same Jesus who encountered the woman at the well met Maribel where she was—hurting, longing, and trapped in that UP prison. He drew near enough to hear her repentance. Jesus wiped away her past sins, healed her marriage, and began to execute his plan for her life. Maribel is currently a vibrant life coach, ministry leader, and speaker to crowds who want to know how to be freed from their own UP. And as Maribel now dances to the new beat of her love for Jesus, he has rewarded her with wisdom. She uses her insights to illustrate the victory over her UP and ushers folks up and out of their own tainted pasts.

Trina also stepped away from the familiar. God sent her a man who helped her imagine a different future for herself. A man who loved her enough to marry her and helped her leave behind her life as an exotic dancer. Then she met the Man who made her dreams come true—Jesus. He scooped her up and wiped away her stains of insecurity and shame. Jesus clothed her with his robe of compassion and grace. Trina now is a gentle lady, a mom, a grandmother, and a church singer who is always ready to sing about Jesus' redeeming love.

And me, I learned that God's divine affection by sending Jesus makes up for any of my *papi's* deficiencies. Not only that, but forgiveness and understanding shine through the new life God has given me. When I thirst for words of reassurance and love, my heavenly *Papi* pours them out in quantities that make my heart overflow. My husband filled my life as my partner and companion. And Jesus filled my heart's void.

What happened to Nancy? After she let go of her past and said "yes" to Jesus, he said to her, "Come, sweet daughter, I'm taking you on a trip." He has taken her to more than 57 countries around the world. As the global ambassador for the largest evangelical ministry in the world, Nancy uses her dynamic style and passion to proclaim God's healing power and goodness in the midst of addiction. And she chose to devote her life to the One who guaranteed he would never leave her and would love her enough to die for her. She travels all over the world, speaking to thousands of women who are stuck in the UP mode, to youth to help them avoid the pitfalls of life, and to folks who are trapped in defeat.

Stubborn?...Me?

None of these *chicas'* transformations was immediate. In some cases the preparation was done in the slow cooker. Why? Because sometimes we are stuck in the seat of stubbornness. And because the Lord knows that, Jesus gives us a vivid example.

In John 4, Jesus meets a woman at a well. She isn't named in the story, and I dare say I know the reason. That woman has your name and mine. She is every woman who walks through life thirsty for freedom from the past. She is each woman who scratches her head wondering where's happiness? Where's peace, complete and lasting?

When Jesus met her, he didn't ask her about her past or her childhood, whether it was happy, sad, or traumatic. Instead, he offered something life-changing. He offered the life-giving water that flows from him and quenches parched souls and washes ugly pasts. Hearing about this living water, her reaction is similar to what yours and mine would be. With bubbling excitement, she asks him for that water. But Jesus, probably with a sweet and gentle voice, says, "Go, call your husband and come back."

"I have no husband," she replied.

Jesus said to her, "You are right when you say you have no husband. The fact is, you have had five husbands, and the man you now have is not your husband. What you have just said is quite true" (John 4:16-18).

The Bible doesn't say she blushed with embarrassment or turned her eyes away from his in shame. Instead, she changed the subject and questioned something that had nothing to do with what Jesus offered. She asked about the correct place to worship according to their traditions. And then she did something we've all done from time to time. She missed the obvious. While she stood before Jesus, the Christ, face to face, in the clarity of the bright noon sun, she said, "I know that Messiah (called Christ) is coming. When he comes, he will explain everything to us."

It was then that Jesus declared clearly, "I who speak to you am he" (John 4:25-26).

What's the matter with her? She's talking to the Christ himself, but she doesn't recognize him. *Un momento.* Let's be easy on her. We do the very same thing. As you read these lines, Christ is saying the very same thing to you: "*Muchacha,* I'm here beside you. My Holy Spirit is present, whispering to you. So why are you still waiting for that moment when you'll encounter me? I'm face to face with you, offering freedom from those chains and longing, offering to fill you with the peace your heart thirsts for." And if you decide to take off those dark sunglasses, lean forward, and with eyes big as your *abuela's* dinner plates, you'll recognize Jesus. Maybe you'll gasp as you ask, "Is that you, J-E-S-U-S?"

Then it hits you—and you know. It is he, real and alive.

After you swallow hard and, with passion in your voice, conviction in your heart, and empty of human apprehensions, you declare, "Lord, I believe you. I really and truly do, because you said, 'Very truly I tell you, whoever hears my word and believes him who sent me has eternal life and will not be judged but has crossed over from death to life'" (John 5:24).

The past is dead, but the future is alive, vibrant, and waiting for you and me.

It's Your Turn

Okay, *chica*, no more analyzing. It's your turn to open your heart, part those red lips and with shyness stuffed back in your purse, declare with all the honesty your *abuela* taught you, "Lord, it's you and me. I cancel my membership in the UP club because I'm moving on, dancing together with you to the rhythm of your promises of healing and restoration. I'm tired of living in the desert—the wilderness of my pain."

God's answer is sweet yet direct: "Forget the former things; do not dwell on the past. See, I am doing a new thing! Now it springs up; do you not perceive it? I am making a way in the wilderness and streams in the wasteland" (Isaiah 43:18-19).

That stream, fresh and inviting, calls you and me. No more *vida loca*, just *vida de amor*—a life of love. No more dragging smelly garbage behind us, just the sweet fragrance of freedom—the kind that sets us free from our weaknesses, flaws, and failures. Let's begin again. It's easier now. We'll lift our chins high, bring those shoulders back, and loop our arms around Jesus. While dressed in outfits given to us by the King of kings, we hold on tight and take firm steps into tomorrow.

And with that fresh passion that now swirls in our Latina hearts, we call out, "C'mon everybody, grab your maracas. Time to celebrate the party of life. No more holding back. Freedom is ours, and we have a new beginning. We follow Jesus whom we love with all our hearts, with all our souls, and with all our minds."

3
I Hate It When God Is Silent

Fear that God won't answer
adds anguish to pain.

Amiga, go ahead, take a peek in the mirror. If you've been able to
let go of that ugly past, no doubt, you're looking younger and more
alive now. There may be moments when troubling memories will
come back, but there's no need to panic. The past hasn't disappeared. What *has* vanished is the grip your past had on you. So,
muchacha, grab your *café con leche* and settle into that soft couch.
It's time to see what happens in the present and discover what to
expect for the future.

Like the catchy salsa rhythm flowing through our Latina bloodstream, problems flow through our days—bad news from the doctor, financial fears, battles that drain us, conflicts that keep us awake
at night, and jammed schedules that leave us fatigued. And when all
those stresses press down on us, we let our shoulders sag, swallow
hard, and do what Mami taught us. We pray. We ask and plead,
"*Por favor*, God…will you change my circumstances, answer my
prayer, or send healing, *pronto*?"

When God seems silent, we indulge in large portions of added
stress. Tension makes us squirm with impatience, and we pace the
floor. We can't even bite our nails because they're acrylic! So we
sweat waiting and waiting. "*Caramba!* When is God going to give
me the solution?"

A woman in the Bible named Hannah lived through some of

27

this. Hannah and Peninnah were both married to the same man. While Peninnah had given her husband children, Hannah had none. "Because the Lord had closed Hannah's womb, her rival [Peninnah] kept provoking her in order to irritate her. This went on year after year" (1 Samuel 1:6-7).

It Never Seems to End

Year after year of mocking and unanswered prayer? Goodness gracious, that's way too long for this *chica*. I wonder if you and I would endure like Hannah. Would we control the irritation that sizzles and continue to pray with the serenity of a tulip? *No creo*, I don't think so. If you and I were in her place, the story might have been different. One day, if Peninnah crossed the line and mocked our misery a bit too much, we might have stomped over to her, dropped our wrinkled tissue on the ground, and slapped Peninnah's chubby cheek.

Or maybe we wouldn't have done that. Instead, we might have taken another big swallow of self-pity. And in the hot sun, we would've sunk lower into the stone bench beside our tent and, with tears of envy wetting our cheeks, we'd have watched Peninnah's kids giggle and play.

The fact is, this kind of thing still happens today. We all have Peninnahs. They're our rivals who taunt us, waiting for us to snap and lash out. They're the ones who make us want to flop down on our beds and sink our faces in our pillows and shout, "I'm done praying…I can't take it anymore!"

But being the calm, mature, Christian *chicas* we are, we suppress all that stuff and avoid that irrational behavior. Outwardly, we appear to be in control, because we read the Bible and believe in God's power and love. We even grin with satisfaction because we mastered the art of memorizing Bible verses.

The Commotion of Our Emotion

But even when we memorize all the Scriptures, even when we believe all the right things, there can still be a problem. Sometimes we have all the facts in our brain, but we're missing God's wisdom in our hearts. I'm talking about that divine wisdom that goes before us to recognize and identify the troublemakers.

The troublemakers I'm talking about are called negative emotions. Although our emotions are part of the way God has created us, sometimes the hot emotions fill our Latina hearts and plug our ears, preventing us from hearing the answer. Not so subtly, these emotions are playing the bongos of discouragement, doubt, or defeat. They reinforce the negative, telling us it's okay to be anxious for an answer, impatient if it doesn't happen in our timing, worried that nothing will change, and fearful God isn't listening at all.

We often give negative emotions a power they don't deserve. And, if we're not careful, sigh…they might win. I hate to admit it, but I'm familiar with this. Many times I've forged onto the battlefield in my high heels, filled with foolish confidence in myself, but underestimating the power of destructive emotions.

Remember when I related the time I lost my eyesight completely? After that happened, I gave one last sob of desperation, and then found the secure arms of Jesus waiting to guide me. That was a new beginning for me. And as his brand new child, giggling with excitement, I set off anew—thinking nothing could discourage me or set me back.

Huh! How feeble could my thinking be? This over-enthusiastic Latina didn't know the force of her sinful nature. But *amigas*, that's the reality of life. No matter how holy we say we are, sin and destructive emotions come in pairs like our pantyhose. And the struggle to overcome them is fierce.

Poor Hannah knew this, but she stood firm against sin and against those sorry emotions, especially when Peninnah's torments jabbed at her. And daring to compare myself to Hannah, I also had my own Peninnah who irritated me. She emphasized discouragement. She said: "You'll never be able to care for your three-, five-, and seven-year-old *niños*." I believed her because often I would reach for them, but I didn't know exactly where they were. I wanted to help them with their homework, but couldn't.

Insecurity about my marriage also increased my anxiety. What will your husband do? How could he love a blind woman? He married a healthy, attractive woman who was able to take on the world. And look at you now! Part of me agreed with my Peninnah's assertion. My marriage became frightfully shaky, and *mi esposo* became distant, confused, and discouraged about our future together. (There are lots of yucky details about this; I'll spell it all out in later chapters.)

Self-pity also fired up: What will happen to you when your kids are grown? Will you ever be productive? What a burden you will be for others. My parents worried about me; my friends were clueless about how to help. And for me, job opportunities were as rare as book clubs for the blind.

Amiga, do you see how emotions can stomp through your senses and bring the rotten kind of thinking that is so very far from God's truth? That's why some of us face defeat. We encounter a sense of gloom because we are living only to have that one desperate prayer answered, to have that problem resolved, and to make things better, changed, or healed. We plead for that night and day. We want so badly to find that peace—the peace we think we'll have only when the prayer is answered.

And when no answer comes, or when God's answer is not what we'd hoped, we add inadequacy to the haunting pile of emotions. We wonder what we're doing wrong. Are we not praying with the right words? Are we not praying long enough, or with sufficient fervor, or spirituality? And we want to scream, "Will somebody teach me how to do it right?"

The Secret That Whispers

I had been wrestling with those very emotions as I asked for healing and begged God to let me see again. But in the midst of my prayer time, life called.

"Mommy, I want a drink," my three-year-old called out from the kitchen. I brushed away my tears with the back of my hand. And with my fingertips, I followed the bed to the wooden footboard, then took a few steps to the dresser, and followed it to the door. I groped my way to the kitchen as I'd done for months. My three small sons had grown accustomed to my new way of navigating through the house.

But I still stumbled as I tried to make my way. And moments like these nudged me to keep asking, "Lord, *cuando*, when will that healing happen?" This was another turning point for this *chica*. I found the secret that few know, and even fewer remember: In order to sing victory over harmful emotions and stinking self-pity, we *have* to recognize how far God has already brought us. Only then can we begin to see how far God will take us.

So how far had God brought me anyway? I'll play the film of my restoration for you. Here's the first scene: When blindness first entered into my life, I saw myself like the blob of fat my *abuela* carved off the chicken before cooking it. I felt worthless, ugly, and fit to be discarded. That view of myself taunted me. I'd always expected to live a life of success. I'd delighted in the pretty side of life. But blindness changed all that. Life wasn't pretty anymore. It was dark, scary, and uncertain. But in the midst of my feelings of inadequacy and self-deprecating thoughts, God stepped in and decided to speed up the restoration.

Hell Isn't for Me

First, God noted how lost and confused I was. *So,* God probably thought, *we need to begin at the beginning with this chica.* So that's what God did. The first step was to make me an offer. The offer to save me from the fire of hell. Hell? That couldn't be. For me? No way. I was the good *muchacha* who attended church each Sunday, confessed my sins from time to time, and was even nice to those telemarketers. Hell wasn't for me. That hot place was for those who sinned really, really big. But God knew my ignorance and offered to save my soul from eternal doom. God said, "Here's my son Jesus. Will you accept him? He's the one who already died for those sins. He conquered the effects of those negative emotions, and demolished the barrier of sin that could've barred you from heaven. And best of all, Jesus is alive and active, waiting for your answer."

When my heart heard this sweet invitation, what do you think I did? I said an emphatic, *"Sí!"* to Jesus. And with the same fervor with which I'd cried to him for a miracle, I swung open the door of my heart. I said, "Come in. What you'll see is a mess. It's chaotic, really. Things are zany because of what I've experienced. I've had no time to clean up. Dishes with caked-on anguish are still in the sink. The floor has crumbs of uncertainty, and fear has left stains on the couch where I cried so often. But Jesus, come in anyway."

I didn't know this, but he had been waiting at the door with mop and bleach in hand, eager to rid me of the stains of my sins. And with a gentle voice, Jesus assured me. "You know, dear *chica*, here's my Word and the promise that I will be the lamp unto your feet, and the light unto your path. And beyond that, I guarantee eternal life, the kind of life that never ends."

With a clean heart, I smiled big for the first time since my eyesight left.

Remembering how Jesus saved me, how he changed my think-ing, and how he lifted me out of the darkness gave me 20/20 spir-itual vision for the future. Now, I am content in waiting for heal-ing. And I know that he will hold tighter should I fall, when storms draw near, or when life crumbles before me. That's why my prayers play the melody of reassurance, repeating the chorus: In the very same way Jesus carried you from yesterday's pain, he'll carry you to tomorrow's victory.

Party with Me

With that song of triumph carrying us into the future, it's time to call our *amigas* to the party of celebration. The guests need to be invited: willingness to accept God's truth, enthusiasm to overcome gloom, encouragement when we see no changes, peace to over-come doubt, and joy to renew our strength.

But even as I prepared for the party, setting the table with food and standing on a chair to hang the *piñata*, the inevitable question came: "Janet, what's with the celebrating? Do you really think God answered your prayer? You still aren't able to see."

It's a logical question. But the answer is simple: I asked for what I wanted, but God gave me what I needed. You read that right. *Claro*, of course, I wanted to see again. But even more desperately, I was longing for security, hungering for genuine confidence, and thirsting for peace. While sighted, I had a problem. I dashed about seeking satisfaction and significance, hoping to find it in college degrees, meaningful relationships, a nice house, fancy cars, and other junk. But that deep, deep sense of peace and security was as elusive as snow in Puerto Rico's summer.

And when I opened my spiritual eyes, it was there—ready and prepared for me.

What about those moments I thought God was silent? Or even

worse, what about when I imagined him with arms crossed, shaking his head, "No. I'm deaf to your prayers. You'll be blind the rest of your life." Was that really true?

No, *Señor!* With passionate love for me, God had been working tirelessly the whole time, crafting the answer. As sure as I'm pressing the keys on this keyboard, I was certain God was responding to my prayer, because of the assurance found in the Word: "This is the confidence we have in approaching God: that if we ask anything according to his will, he hears us. And if we know that he hears us—whatever we ask—we know that we have what we asked of him" (1 John 5:14-15).

There you have it, the truth right from God's Word. You and I can have confidence approaching God when two things happen: First, when Jesus fills our hearts; and second, when we align our requests with his will. The answer is certainly on the way, and God is the one who sets the time on his divine stopwatch.

In my case, God may have set it for a little longer than you might expect. As of this writing, it's been more than two decades. *Sigo esperando*—I'm still waiting. But *amigas*, the waiting is glorious, rich, and amazingly filled with joy.

This Way to the Waiting Room

Did I really say that? That waiting is glorious? *Claro*, it is. Joyful? I know it might sound a bit bizarre. The notion that waiting can be a time to celebrate might make your penciled eyebrows arch in surprise. But it's true. The waiting room is where it all happens.

There are two groups of people. One group exudes peace even in difficult circumstances. The other group includes the folks who go into hysterics over small things like a long line at the post office. The difference between the two kinds of people is the way they decorate their waiting rooms.

No one has ever gone through life receiving an automatic answer to every request. You and I are no exception. We've all had to step in that waiting room of life.

And while in there, I suggest we do what Hannah did when she stepped into her own waiting room. Like her, we need to open the windows to let the light of hope come in. Hannah must have taken classes to know how to best decorate it. All over the room, she splashed hues of perseverance. Years went by, God didn't answer, yet still she prayed. Peninnah mocked. Hannah prayed. Other women had enough kids to fill two tents. She had none. But still she prayed. Her hubby told her to get a life. She prayed. Her appetite left. She still prayed.

For her, the-prayer-in-waiting was for a baby. What about you? What is the one thing that keeps you from saying, "I'm totally happy with my life?" If that "something" hasn't shown up yet, God may have also reserved a seat in the waiting room of his heart for you.

And while you pace back and forth, wringing your manicured hands, God is watching. God sees how you feverishly sprint to the mailbox to see if the answer has come. God notices how your impatience makes you so nervous you dart to the fridge and nearly eat an entire rum cake, and how worry makes you toss during sleepless nights.

I understand your worry and impatience. I've been there. But *caramba!* Why didn't anyone tell me God was at work the whole time?

Ouch! That Chiseling Hurts

In case no one told you either, let me tell you now: God is at work. And since you're smarter than I am, I hope you'll find it easier than I did to give one last heaving sigh and look up. Take a deep breath.

Put that cake back in the fridge. There's no room for anxiety, stress, or tension because each moment that goes by, each day that passes, God's hands are at work.

You may clean those eyeglasses, put them back on, and lean forward to take a closer look at the circumstance you want changed. And, heavens, you can see no change at all. Before impatience gives you indigestion, consider that faith doesn't gauge visible changes, but measures the depth of our belief. Trust that the God of the universe is working—reshaping our broken hearts, chiseling away stuff that shouldn't be there, dabbing color in worn out areas, and polishing our lives to shine with his grace. A bit uncomfortable? Yes, but so needed.

It doesn't matter what you are seeking. Whatever your request, the work you need to do can be found right behind your left set of ribs.

Here's an example of how it works. My friend was in the workshop under the hands of the Master. But she had to begin by taking a humility pill in order to sit still. "My husband makes me so angry. I'm losing my patience," she said. Her husband had been aloof, distant, and sometimes emotionally removed from her. To add to her loneliness, he kept certain information from her, such as how much money he made. He treated her as if she were a stranger. For years, she asked the Lord to change him, to soften his heart, and to create a desire in him to go back to church. She pleaded that God would make him more attentive to her and that he'd show her a bit of affection.

Then one day, ouch! God sanded a bit into her pride. She'd been sure hubby was the one who needed the work and the transformation. She had walked down the true-Christian aisle. In fact, she was the pillar in her church—active in ministry, loved by all, admired for her attributes as a teacher. Why in the world would God expect her to change? On the contrary, she felt God should be rewarding her for her diligence in serving him

Goodness, that seems confusing to me, too. We all know *mujeres* who seem to do everything right, yet still have problems, difficult moments, and relationships that don't work. Why would God expect them to change?

"You know what I did?" my friend told me. "I offered to watch TV with him."

I knew that was big, because her husband watched programs that bored her silly. But she wanted to show him she cared. She held back criticism. And, another huge step was to force herself to be silent and let him talk. When he suggested something, rather than rolling her eyes, she smiled. And when he came home, she initiated affection. For years and years, she had asked God to change him. But God did something different in response to her prayer. God changed her.

She called me the other night. "You won't believe what he did. He bought me a new watch. I've been asking for that for so long. And…" She chuckled. "He wants to start having date nights. He's sixty-seven and wants date nights. Can you believe it?"

The changes we desperately cry for require a time-out. We need to give it enough time to let God work—are you ready?—not on the circumstance, but on us. The process burns a little, but it's needed. Necessary like *abuela's sopa de pollo*, she takes it off the burner only when it's cooked, soft and ready.

It could be that we need to place that doubt, apprehension, anger, and anxiety on the burner and let it evaporate in the steam of God's grace. Then, *amiga*, and only then, you'll hear from heaven, you'll see the results, and you'll delight in the rich times while you wait for the answer.

But That's Not the Answer I Ordered

Intelligent *chicas* that we are, we know God's answer might not fit our designed format. My friend's marriage improved, Hannah finally had her baby, but I'm still blind. God's answer came to me, but not by way of restoring my physical eyesight. The answer came in freedom from painful insecurity, from shallow thinking, and from anxiety about tomorrow.

So far in this book, I've been extremely honest with you—and I won't stop now. Do I wish to see again? *Sí*. After twenty-four years of living without sight, the desire to see a sunrise or my grandchildren's smile still peeks in from time to time. It could be that the first thing I see when God's loving hand restores my retina will be his divine face in the glory of heaven. Or if God restores my sight while I'm still on earth, and I glance at my reflection in the mirror …a huge gasp would escape from my lips because shock of all shocks—I don't look thirty-one anymore!

Whatever God chooses, *está bien*; it's okay because in the meantime, I'm busy, really busy. I'm decorating my waiting room. I set a small table and placed a crystal pitcher filled with refreshing faith, and a note to remind me to refill whenever it gets low. Beside it, I have a soft chair of expectation. And while snuggled in its softness, I relax, expecting not so much to be healed, but to lean on God when my world gets shaky, to hear God's whispers of encouragement and strength, and to let God restore my passion to keep going when the world says it's a shame to be blind.

I even dare to expect God's abundant provision to provide for every need this blind *chica* has. And that includes technology such as this screen reader for my computer, enabling me to craft insights for you.

God Collects Them All

I can guess that you might be wrinkling your nose at my assertion. After all, you rumble, I have no clue about your situation: The fact that your child is dying, or your husband just walked out, or cancer has entered your life.

Good news. I may not know, but God specializes in accompanying us through times of agony, sorrow, or fear. And when you sit on the bed in the middle of yet another sleepless night, when your lips quiver, your mind is mush with confusion, and tears of heartache and desperation trickle down your cheeks, God will be there to catch them. The psalmist declared that the Lord collects each tear in a bottle (see Psalm 56:8, KJV). So, God knows the distress our tears contain, the heartache that taints them, and the hopelessness that keeps them flowing. Our God is aware of it all. And at a moment that's neither too late nor a second too soon, the door to the waiting room will open, and we will hear God say, "You waited, and I answered."

But what's important, so very important, is that until then, God will restore the joy we've forgotten, the security we've left behind, and the peace that has become foreign. Each moment will be another firm step forward. And *amiga*, our days will be bearable, because as sure as dawn ends the night, we can be certain of God's answer, because it's found not in the prayer while we ask, but in the peace while we wait.

4
Financial Frenzy

No amount of fear can increase
our bank accounts, and no amount of losses
can decrease God's provision.

Amigas, we're strange creatures sometimes. We are sitting on the couch, sipping our espressos, and feeling good about ourselves. Then, when we least expect it, shocking news makes us choke. And quicker than we can say *"que pasó?"* our emotions shoot out from our every nerve. They go wild like the chicken after *abuela* snapped its head off.

And then we end up directing those negative emotions toward whoever ends up in our path. That's what I did. After some discouraging news sent my emotions ricocheting out of control. I looked in my *esposo's* direction and wanted to shout, "I hate you for putting us in this mess."

I really didn't hate Gene. But I did hate the situation.

Here's how it began:

A couple of friends had repeatedly asked Gene if he would manage the finances of their small company. They were struggling and needed help. And being the softhearted guy that he is, he was tempted.

"Honey, are you sure?" I asked. "Can't they find someone else to help? Besides, you already have a good job with good pay and benefits. Do you really want to leave that?"

"I have to help them," he said. "They need someone with financial experience. Don't worry. We'll be okay."

Maybe we would; maybe we wouldn't. But watching him leave a secure position with a large company to work in a small, struggling, and unstable company gave me indigestion.

But really, what choice did I have? C'mon, *chica*, I said to myself. I had to support his decision because I was his wife, right? And, after all, his willingness to do anything to help others made him extra charming and lovable.

So while I pouted at his resolve, he took off to his new work. Six months into the job, it became very clear that the company's financial state was ugly—really ugly. "There's no cash flow to meet payroll," he told me.

I knew that already, because I'd seen the decrease in his paycheck. I gave a fake smile and resisted the temptation to yell out, "I told you so."

The small company was in huge trouble, more serious than he could handle. And as the debt to the federal government, vendors, and suppliers grew, so did my resentment about the whole situation.

But, as always, *amigas*, God had a lesson in store—for me.

One day Gene came home from work, and I could tell he had bad news. After dinner, we took a walk. He was silent at first. It was the kind of silence that precedes nothing good.

"What went on today?" I said.

He let out a big sigh. "We need to close the company, shut down business."

Shut down? Did he mean they were closing the doors, and we'd see no more paychecks? He was telling me he was out of a job.

But oh, dear *muchachas*, that wasn't the worst thing. He cleared his throat as he always did when something bad, something *really* bad, was about to slip from his *gringo* lips.

"There's a 100 percent penalty against us."

I knew the word "penalty" didn't sound good. But I still wasn't sure what he was saying. "What does that mean—'against us'?"

He blew out a deep sigh. "We owe that money."

"The company had made a deal with the IRS to pay in small increments the federal taxes they'd deducted from employees' paychecks. But now, with the company closing, they want the full amount."

I breathed relief. The company wasn't ours, so that meant we weren't involved.

"As the controller…" He cleared his throat again. "I'm personally responsible, along with the president and vice president."

I froze. I could tell by his tone the debt was no small amount.

"That's not fair. How much do they expect us to pay?"

When he said it was a quarter of a million dollars, my stomach cramped. We couldn't pay that off in a lifetime. Although the debt was divided among the three officers of the company, the interest and penalties would add up quickly.

Still in shock, I needed to understand. "That can't be true. Are you sure? Did you research?"

"It's federal law that when you owe FICA taxes, the officers of the company are personally liable."

One of the men responsible had quickly declared bankruptcy. That left the full amount between us and the other man.

"God," I wanted to cry out. "Why did you allow this to happen to us?"

But God's answer didn't come quickly. And the situation was about to get worse. On top of that huge debt, Gene's income stopped.

We hired an attorney to defend us. And goodness, his fees nearly made me nauseous. But having no other option, we used most of the funds in our savings account to pay him. And the rest went to make the initial payments on the debt. The savings for our kids' college diminished to nothing, as did our other bank accounts.

And months later, with Gene without an income, we had nothing left. Every dollar in every account and every expense, from the mortgage to dry-cleaning bills, had to be disclosed to the IRS. They used this information to decide the amount we needed to live on and took the rest.

The only thing we had was my income, which didn't even cover the utility bills. We had to secure funds from bank loans and from relatives and friends to make some payments. But the money we borrowed didn't even come close to the balance owed.

I hated the unfairness. And over and over again, I reviewed the details while I lay awake at night. Having little strength, I coveted David's courage. I saw images of Goliath, with the letters *IRS* tattooed on his large forehead, slowly stomping toward us. With massive hands, he scraped every dollar from us.

"Can I have a Nintendo for Christmas?" Our oldest son was thirteen at the time, and this was a popular game among kids his age.

"This Christmas is going to be different," I said without going into much detail. Lots of things would be different. In fact, we even had to stop the not-so-happy meals at McDonalds.

They Don't Even Go to Church

Have you been there, *muchacha*? Has an unfair, out-of-your-control situation ever turned your world upside down? You did nothing to deserve this scenario. And trying to sort through the chaos, you think you're doing the right thing. But the deep unfairness still slaps your powdered cheek. No matter what you do, nothing seems to work. To make your pain sharper, you look around and see other people living fine lives—undisturbed, happy, and prosperous. And to add to the indignation, they don't even go to church. "What's up with that, God?" you want to ask. Undeserved consequences bring a deep resentment that burns more than *abuela*'s jalapeño peppers.

Then the biggie comes to visit—guilt. In my case, I started to wonder if I should have been stronger with hubby and refused to let him leave his other job.

A bit of rebellion slithered through. Why should I be expected to support his decisions? Didn't God know a man like Gene could think upside down and backward sometimes?

We're nutty *chicas*, aren't we? We like to put the blame on others—our spouses, especially. And in a shameful kind of way, we find a tad of satisfaction in doing so. But doing that is not the answer.

The solution is hard to swallow: We should lift our heads high and tell ourselves we're godly women. And over and over again, we repeat to ourselves that we're capable of facing the toughest hardships. And with a glow in our complexions, we vow to over-come them no matter what.

I tried that. I really did. I took on the daily chores with a style described in Proverbs 31.

But this Proverbs 31 woman turned ugly when Gene checked the mail one day and ripped open an envelope. "It's from the IRS."

Anger simmered in my chest. My nerves got tight and my fore-head got sweaty.

He read the contents in silence. "We have to go to court again."

He was required to appear in court to appeal his case. I chided myself for allowing a bit of hope to shine through. The outcome never brought good news. Instead, each appearance generated a hefty bill from the attorney.

Remember Where We Came From

I flinched as I thought about all the sacrifices my parents had made for years to bring my brother and me to the United States to find opportunities for us and our children. And now, rather than prosperity, we were facing financial doom.

I confided in my mom. And in her Bolivian way of thinking, she reminded me: "Remember when we lived in La Paz and your father and I worked so hard to get the money and documents to come here?"

Sí, I remembered—the sacrifice, the struggle to meet the U.S. immigration requirements, and the meager meals we ate because we had so little money. And once in the United States, we faced adjustments, hard times, and ridicule. But we made slow progress until we reached success.

How silly and strange. Gene and I were also in the country of financial stress and wishing to enter the land of prosperity. But the border was closed, and we were stuck in a dead end of impossibilities, unfairness, and oppression. We would have done anything to cross the border and be set free from the debt that hovered over us like a ruthless dictator.

"Your papi and I could've trusted in our own way of doing things," Mami said. "We could've crossed the border with no papers and hoped to have a happy life. But if you trust in your own ways and not in God, you'll never know prosperity with peace."

Mami was right. While they were in Bolivia, they didn't place their trust in the opportunities available in the United States to bring prosperity. Instead, they trusted in God's ways to lead them in the right path. And had God kept us in Bolivia, God would've provided for our needs there too.

So what was wrong with us? We had made that grand mistake. And then, while in the land of debt, we trusted in our attorney to get us out of this mess. We trusted in our financial creativity to secure loans. We put our trust in the IRS agent's mercy to give us a little break.

I knew what the Scriptures said: "Trust in the LORD with all your heart and lean not on your own understanding" (Proverbs 3:5).

But stubborn with my complaints, I wanted to shout, "God, do you know how hard is to trust when each step we take sinks us deeper into the quicksand of financial ruin?"

God seemed silent and distant. And even when the prayers of our friends and family joined ours, they seemed futile and hopeless.

Obey? Not Now!

Tough financial situations touched even *chicas* in the Bible. Ruth knew this kind of stress. Remember when she pleaded with Naomi to let her accompany her to the land of Judah?

Ruth had no idea what awaited her, but she knew she wanted to be with Naomi. *Chica*, I can relate. Can you? Ruth entered a foreign land where she was a stranger. In these unfamiliar surroundings, she didn't find friends. Instead she found folks who pointed at her as someone different.

But Ruth had a secret—her commitment to obey.

Obey....hmmm. That word has a sour taste in our mouths because we live in a time where assertiveness and self-assurance rule. And maybe in the twenty-first century, no woman with a hint of pride would do what Naomi asked Ruth to do:

> One day Ruth's mother-in-law Naomi said to her, "My daughter, I must find a home for you, where you will be well provided for. Now Boaz, with whose women you have worked, is a relative of ours. Tonight he will be winnowing barley on the threshing floor. Wash, put on perfume, and get dressed in your best clothes. Then go down to the threshing floor, but don't let him know you are there until he has finished eating and drinking. When he lies down, note the place where he is lying. Then go and uncover his feet and lie down. He will tell you what to do." (Ruth 3:1-4)

Going to Higher Places

Amigas, would you agree that's a tough thing to do? If my mother-in-law gave me those instructions, tradition or not, I'd have to question the request, or at least negotiate a bit. Get dressed up, spray on some floral perfume, and sneak into the sleeping roll of a man who is probably stinky from sweating all day? *No gracias!*

But Ruth has a nobler attitude. And it's a good thing she did, because the outcome is sweet:

> "I will do whatever you say," Ruth answered. So she went down to the threshing floor and did everything her mother-in-law told her to do.
>
> When Boaz had finished eating and drinking and was in good spirits, he went over to lie down at the far end of the grain pile. Ruth approached quietly, uncovered his feet and lay down. In the middle of the night, something startled the man; he turned—and there was a woman lying at his feet!
>
> "Who are you?" he asked.
>
> "I am your servant Ruth," she said. "Spread the corner of your garment over me, since you are a guardian-redeemer of our family."
>
> "The LORD bless you, my daughter," he replied. "This kindness is greater than that which you showed earlier: You have not run after the younger men, whether rich or poor. And now, my daughter, don't be afraid. I will do for you all you ask." (Ruth 3:5-11)

Imagine that! Boaz had a great-looking, pretty-smelling gal in his bed. Yet he was honorable, honest, caring, and ever so genuine. From the rest of the story, we know Ruth becomes his wife.

But here's the thing. Ruth could've held on to her pride and chosen to disobey Naomi's silly-sounding order. But had she disobeyed, she probably would still be scraping the leftovers from the fields and be stuck with a diet of dried-up grains.

Ruth's obedience took her to higher places. As Boaz's cherished wife, she then possessed the land, large and abundant, the riches, possessions, and inheritance he provided.

But wait a minute. It wasn't Boaz who provided all this. It was God. God was the one who had all this planned for Ruth and her future. And what a future it was! She became nothing less than an ancestor of Jesus, the Redeemer of the world.

To Pay or to Obey

So what does that have to do with the ugly financial situation that my hubby and I were facing? Actually, *amiga*, Ruth's example has the answer.

We were unable to meet the IRS demands to pay. But we *could* meet God's request to obey. Like Ruth, we'd entered a different land and become part of a different group. We were now counted among the people who had created their own financial doom by squandering their money. They quickly cross the green light only to find their finances in the red. How unfair it was that we were stuck in that group! But once I stopped whining, the truth emerged. How you get into the money mess doesn't matter. The only important thing is to follow Ruth's example to obey.

One night, the kids were in bed, and we again sat at the kitchen table. Although I wanted a break from the reminder of the gloom that dampened our peace, we needed to figure out what the next step would be.

Did I mention that the IRS didn't consider tithing a "living necessity"? The tithing amount couldn't come from the funds assigned for utilities, insurance, or other bills. Often, the funds were so tight that we couldn't pay the increasing utilities. At the risk of sounding a bit self-righteous, I'll tell you that we chose to rob funds from the food budget to tithe. Beginning the day we married, tithing had become a normal, expected, and non-negotiable habit of ours. I say habit, because up to then, we had no idea of the implications of obeying this direct mandate from God.

I blush as I admit this, but we often didn't bring our tithing with cheerful faces. So in that department, when Scripture said God loves a "cheerful giver" (2 Corinthians 9:7), we needed an increased amount of grace! But one ingredient that made obedience more complete was to "bring" it to God's house—not to send it, mail it, or postpone it until we happened to be near a church. "'Bring the whole tithe into the storehouse, that there may be food in my house. Test me in this,' says the LORD Almighty" (Malachi 3:10).

Test the Lord Almighty? I can't imagine anyone who would be bold enough to do that. But *chicas*, the Lord knows how stubborn we can be. And God is aware of our insistence on holding onto what we see as logical, acceptable, and sensible. Would you blame me if I had looked the other way when the collection basket came by? I was tempted to "forget" to pull the envelope out of my purse and tear up the check when I got home. But *caramba*! God would have seen that, too.

Although we know the right thing to do, temptation is sometimes as inviting as cheesy tostadas fresh out of the oven.

We counted on the influence of others, too. We almost believed that bankruptcy could have been the next step. In fact, many advised us to follow that route. But God's view is clear and direct. "Test me, try me, just wait and see." That's what the Spirit seemed to be saying to us. Sunday after Sunday, we brought our heavy hearts, our sometimes-crabby kids, and our tithing envelope to church.

Proverbs says, "Honor the Lord with your wealth, with the first-fruits of all your crops; then your barns will be filled to overflowing, and your vats will brim over with new wine" (Proverbs 3:9-10). The barns of that day were like banks today. So I looked up. "Lord, we didn't need our bank account to overflow, just to show a positive balance for a change. Give us a tiny bit of hope—a sign you're up there listening to us."

I had that kind of conversation with God often. Sometimes the conversations were quite intense. From time to time I'd remind the Lord, "You allowed me to be sightless, yet you opened the way for me to work. Can you show me another miracle?"

Then I bargained with God. "If you resolve this for us, I commit to work just for you."

Goodness, desperation can cause us to say and do crazy things. But who could blame me? The clock was ticking and the debt getting bigger, so it seemed reasonable to ask God to hurry and wave a hand over the situation and clear the mess.

Perfect Timing

But leaning on the realities we can see gives us a different view. How wonderful that God watches to see how our faith will endure, how our trust in the Scriptures will shape our thinking, and how our commitment to God's commandments will direct our steps.

Months had passed when Gene came home one day and said, "The attorney called. The IRS is ready for a settlement."

I took a deep breath. "For how much?"

"We have to go and talk to him."

His secretary shooed us to the attorney's office. As usual, Gene described the environment to me, as he did whenever we visited a new place. The large suite was nestled in the most luxurious building in town, with one wall that was nothing but glass overlooking the city and showing a spectacular view. The mahogany desk spread before our attorney was bigger than King Arthur's round table. And I figured we'd probably paid for the fancy antique bookshelves and the set of law books that adorned this exquisite office.

But none of that mattered now. The only thing we needed to know was the amount the IRS would let us pay as a settlement.

I held my breath, and when the final balance slipped from his lips, I sank down in my chair. We would have to seek additional loans to pay it. But a flicker of reassurance came through, because in my mind I saw Goliath pack his stuff and begin to move away. *Gracias*, Lord!

Having a lesser amount to pay, we crafted another plan: Look for a new job for Gene, and tithe. Try to seek more loans and tithe. Seek new ways to cut our expenses and continue to tithe.

While in church, God's message was clear: the Lord had already brought a solution, one we couldn't see. God had marked the steps before we had taken our first one. God had ordered the events even when we anguished over the outcome. And the Lord would also part the Sea should we encounter more troubles.

For a few months, job interviews for Gene came and went. But then one day he had good news: "They called me for a second interview." This time, the offer was solid, and Gene began his new job. But although the compensation was adequate, we had to pay loans to family members first. Meanwhile, the interest in credit cards and bank loans continued to increase.

One night in prayer, Gene and I decided to take a bold step—to ask his employers for an advance. To our delight they accepted, and we were able to pay part of the debt. Although we still owed a large amount, we cheered and praised God in thanksgiving for this provision. We faced years and years of debt. And to this day, this *chica* doesn't know why or how, but we accepted our situation with genuine gratitude.

Boaz Visits Disney

One day, when Gene came home after work, I was stirring rice on the stove. He slid his briefcase on the kitchen counter. "How would you like to move to Florida?"

Florida? The state that has no winters? The idea of leaving the cold weather of St. Louis brought a huge smile and a quick "yes!" from me.

Although he enjoyed his current job, this company also struggled financially. Rumors about the owners closing the doors increased each week. In preparation, Gene had applied for a job in several companies, including Disney World.

The possibility of another job, with more security and better compensation, brought sunshine to our days.

"What did they say?" I asked when he called from Florida after his first interview.

"They didn't offer me the management position," he said.

My shoulders drooped with disappointment. I tried to sound optimistic, but my gloom must have been evident.

"Cheer up," he said. "The VP who interviewed me said my qualifications were more in line with the higher position of director." His voice revealed his excitement. "And they offered it to me."

I saw myself as Ruth when Boaz asked her to be his wife. Her willingness to trust Naomi and Naomi's God brought her to a place beyond her dreams. Her humility and commitment lifted her above poverty. Her diligence paved the way for her new beginning, a joyful and prosperous one. We were living the same transformation as Ruth. A new beginning waited for us too—one that God had for us from the start.

I confess that my silly Latina imagination sometimes gets a bit outrageous. Thinking back on Ruth's story, I pictured the possibilities: What if God had a magical way for a wealthy Ruth and Boaz to meet? Let's say in a fancy dinner held in an opulent dining room? But had God orchestrated their union that way, we'd never have the example of seeing how God's power brings one from tasting *nada* to the sweetness of Prada.

We all face moments when God asks us to step across that bridge. Some are on the *nada* side, lamenting, and cursing the situation. Others are crossing the bridge with lots of trust as they head to the other side. And yet others walk right past the bridge called "obedience."

God uses each threat of foreclosure, unemployment, credit-card debt, unpaid loans, IRS debts, and all that burdens us to make the Spirit's call clearer and louder: Will you trust me and obey me? What we think is impossible, God makes possible. And being blind, I know how tough it is to continue to trust when you don't see the results. But while we're on the bridge, God doesn't work on providing proof but on increasing our faith.

The bridge of obedience proved to be sturdy, trustworthy, and secure. We put our house up for sale and arranged for the movers to come and pack our furniture. I filled our suitcases and gathered our sons, and we headed to Florida to bask in the sunshine of God's provision. The position came with a package that left us in awe. The benefits and stock options exceeded our imagination. Within a year, we'd paid off every loan and credit card. Our savings began to accumulate faster than ever before in all our married life.

Remember when I mentioned that this lesson was meant for me? God knew this episode in our lives long before we encountered it. But through Ruth's story, the Lord showed me the meaning of humility and commitment to the Word. Ruth must have looked back to the time when she had nothing. But now her barn overflowed. And in many ways, ours did too. We had deposited bits of obedience into the bank account of God's Word. While we were sinking in fear, God's grace was already at work. When we didn't have the answers, the Holy Spirit was already molding the perfect solution. When we were filled with doubt, God's mercy overlooked that weakness. When we chose to tithe no matter what, God was gathering blessings. And best of all, when we saw nothing but debt and negative balances, the Lord was already accumulating the perfect provision.

Risking a bit of assumption, I think my story may be similar to yours. We all live in this fallen world, and many of us stare at bills that pile up like garbage after a fiesta. And as expected, the smelly situation brings fret, worry, and sleepless nights. God knew that. And that's probably why the Lord went so far as to say, "Test me in this."

Should you be facing a financial frenzy, go ahead, test God's Word by bringing your first fruits. God will pass the test, guaranteed. And best of all, *amigas*, fear will pass you by, and sweet sleep will visit your nights.

5
Why Me?

Fear is the teakettle where
Satan brews his lies.

My *abuela* came into my bedroom. "Here, *hijita*, sweet honey, drink this. You'll feel better." She put a cup of warm tea in my twelve-year-old hands.

With no heating system to warm us during cold La Paz winter nights, my *abuela* had already piled several wool blankets on me to keep me warm on the outside. Now she was concerned about warming me from the inside!

Moving slowly, Abuela sat on the edge of the bed. I wiggled from under the blankets, sat up, and inhaled the soft aroma of her home-grown herbs. She had steeped leaves from one of the dozens of plants she grew in her garden. Peppermint, chamomile, cat's claw—she had it all. Should anyone in the family mention a slight discomfort, this tiny lady in her knit sweater and long black skirt would shuffle to the kitchen to boil water. She then prepared the perfect tea to cure any ailment from a runny nose to muscle aches. I'm not sure whether it was the tea or the warm smile wrinkling her tanned cheeks that soothed my stomach.

Like me, you may have grown up with home remedies—simple, natural, and inexpensive. That was the way of life back in our country. And through the years, God allowed me to dance the sweet salsa of health. Other than my blindness, the rest of my body worked pretty well...until the day I went for my routine mammogram. No big deal. I went for one every year. And year after year they found nothing.

But this time, the doctor's office called me back for a second test. Her words—"We found something"—took my breath away. They'd probably made a mistake. Surely that's what's happened. I'd always taken good care of myself. I exercised and watched my weight. In fact, friends often teased me about my silly overly cautious eating habits. Goodness gracious, I even opted for organic foods. Why would they find anything wrong?

As is usually the case, the next test wouldn't be for another two weeks. That meant two weeks of torment, uncertainty, and worry. And pretty soon, like water in my *abuela's* teapot, fear was simmering inside of me.

Battling Spiritual Weapons

The day after the doctor's office called, I received a not-too-complimentary note from one of my readers. This man wrote that my newsletter was "a bit on the religious" side. I had written a story about Satan's lies, craftiness, and desire to devour anyone who's not on guard. The reader said he didn't believe in any devil. For a moment, I wanted to follow that notion. No devil? Wouldn't that mean no evil, no darkness? No wrong, pain, or hardships? Instead, the world would be heavenly. We'd see everything to be right, fair, perfect, blameless, and correct.

No, *señorita*, that's not the way things are. With my uncertain diagnosis, I knew life was far from perfect. And during the two weeks I spent waiting for the test results, the reminder of Satan's presence gave off a particularly poignant smell. Most of the time, I was calm and poised on the outside. But inside, the word *cancer* echoed—and I was a spiritual mess.

With a tinge of embarrassment, I admit the devil's crafty attacks caught me off guard. By the time he'd finished thrashing me around emotionally and spiritually, I lay flat on the ground. My hair was going every which way, my eyes were black-and-blue, and I had scratches all over. He'd done his best to tear me down

Aching from Satan's attacks, I had to disagree with my reader. And in doing so, I affirmed what God has told us: the devil is very much alive and ready to devour you and me if we're not cautious. I learned this from experience during those weeks. And because I want you to march on the victory side (as I eventually did), I'm going to describe in detail the weapons he used with me. And dear *chicas*, they're the same the ones he might use with you, too. Here they are:

He Throws His Spear of Doubt.

Worry showed up. But I'd try to remind myself. Hold it. I must be out of my mind to worry. Hadn't I just written a devotional about casting our burdens on the Lord? I'd invited my readers to surrender worry and anxiety. But although others found my insight to be enlightening, I let shameful doubt trickle into me. Why couldn't I shake it off? If God's Word is so powerful, why am I not standing on it instead of tiptoeing through the land of anxiety? I nervously tapped my fingernails on the kitchen counter, wondering if worry would ever leave.

He Infects Our Thoughts.

Whenever my mind was free for even a few seconds, negative possibilities burst in from all directions. Any mention of plans for the future, like celebrating the next grandchild's birthday, sent me spiraling. What if I had terminal cancer and didn't have that long to live? *Stop it*, I'd say to myself. *Those thoughts will make you crazy.* Too late. I was already going a little nutty with concern for my future. My thinking went from, "God is in control and wouldn't allow anything bad to happen to me," to, "I need to write a goodbye letter and leave a legacy to my grandchildren."

Then I made it worse, by comparing myself with others. I looked around. Other people didn't face my ordeal. Of course they had reasons to smile—they could look forward to a healthy future. And me? I was doomed to face cancer in addition to blindness. I wanted to cry out: *Dios mio*? Why me?

He Moves Quickly in Our Weakest Moments.

I chided myself for the self-pity that invaded me from time to time. You know—the "poor me" syndrome that drains our energy, zaps our motivation, and eats up the gusto for life we once knew. I did my best to brush off that feeling. But the more I tried, the more vivid the images of my tragic future became. I was spiritually weak and vulnerable to the enemy's aggression. He probably licked his lips certain I'd be his next prey, as I was already seasoned with discouragement and marinating in negativity. And, *amigas*, this is when he shows up with a boldness you and I can't ignore. Those moments of weakness create familiar and easy-to-invade territory for him, and he goes into action with nauseating finesse.

> Then Jesus was led by the Spirit into the wilderness to be tempted by the devil. After fasting forty days and forty nights, he was hungry. The tempter came to him and said, "If you are the Son of God, tell these stones to become bread."
>
> Jesus answered, "It is written: 'Man does not live on bread alone, but on every word that comes from the mouth of God.'" (Matthew 4:1-4)

If the devil was bold enough to tempt Jesus, he has no qualms about tempting us *chicas*. Have you ever fasted for a blood test? When such tests are over, my stomach's growling can be heard all the way to the parking lot. I rush to devour the first edible thing. And that was after only a few hours of fasting. I cannot imagine forty days and forty nights with no food. Jesus was desperately hungry, probably weak and a bit shaky. And that's when Satan chose to make his attack.

You see, *amiga*, that's where we are when we hear news that rattles our nerves. We're hungry for reassurance, we are weak with fear, and we become shaky at the possible bleak outcome. Satan chooses these weak moments to throw his worst at us.

He Uses Our Emotions to His Benefit.

The devil knows our Latina passion isn't limited to good times. That same gusto and zeal also explode in bad times. We fret beyond comprehension. And our desperate worrying closes the door to God's truth and opens the window to more of Satan's lies. And those lies prevent us from being the loving, calm, understanding *chicas* we want to be. We lash out at those we love. We snap at innocent bystanders. We're rude to those who want to help. And we even blame others for our sad plight. Our negative emotions take over the once-happy *chicas* we've been. By the end of the day, we're emotionally drained, but the memories of those silly reactions dig into us with guilt, robbing us of the sleep we so desperately need.

He Drives a Wild Roller Coaster.

By now, you might be thinking, *"Amiga*, get a life. No one goes through all those stages." But I can assure you that I did. My reasoning was flawed—but real. I'd already faced and adjusted to blindness, but the thought of cancer multiplied my fears. Being the dedicated Christian I try to be, I spent time reading God's Word, and in those moments, calmness filtered through me. I reminded myself that the number of my days is in the Lord's hands. I remembered that God was watching the steps of my journey. God's Spirit would never leave me. God can heal anything. Firmly grasping those truths, I felt a reassuring confidence.

Pretty good stuff, right? I thought so. But the minute I recalled that I might be joining the ranks of friends who have endured the tough cancer journey, all those positive insights evaporated like a puddle in the summer. What can I say? I'm just a sorry *chica*, weaker than most. God's promises lived in my head, but my heart played hostess to Satan's doubts.

He Emphasizes False Security.

Tension filled me as I awaited my diagnosis. Doctors, trained experts in their field, would utter the words that would define my future. As expected, Satan never let up, trying to convince me doctors were the ones who could save me from the disease. He wanted me to believe my destiny, health, and future were in doctors' hands. They were the ones who would read the results, interpret the findings, and wave the wand to heal me. "They have the power," the Enemy whispered.

Amigas, this is nothing new. Satan's ability to divert our trust with his crafty tricks is as alive now as it was when he approached Jesus:

> Then the devil took him to the holy city and had him stand on the highest point of the temple. "If you are the Son of God," he said, "throw yourself down. For it is written: 'He will command his angels concerning you, and they will lift you up in their hands, so that you will not strike your foot against a stone.'"
>
> Jesus answered him, "It is also written: 'Do not put the Lord your God to the test.'" (Matthew 4:5-7)

So there you have it. The lies Satan plants in our heart, the fear that stems from his schemes, and the worry he weaves through our thoughts are all real.

Amiga, take a sip of that *café con leche* and get a bit more comfortable, because we're about to see how God defeats Satan on our behalf.

A Way Out

Paul's *abuela* must have brewed him cups of tea for boldness because he always spoke the truth steeped in God's wisdom: "No temptation has overtaken you except what is common to mankind. And God is faithful; he will not let you be tempted beyond what you can bear. But when you are tempted, he will also provide a way out so that you can endure it" (1 Corinthians 10:13).

How about that? Paul said "when you are tempted" not "if you are tempted." We will face the temptation to fall for the devil's lies. That is inevitable. But so is God's provision for a way to endure them. God always provides a way out.

We need God's power because the lies often pile up on us like heavy wool blankets. God knows that. That's why Jesus didn't call Satan "the father of cruelty" or "the father of malice." Jesus called him "the father of lies" (John 8:44). That name fits him because Satan has custom-designed his lies to fit our every situation.

Forgive my nosy nature, but may I ask what situation it is that you are struggling with now? What has left you uneasy? Maybe it's not a health issue. Instead, it's relationships that are crumbling, finances that leave you frantic, or personal conflicts that frazzle you. Whatever it is, it shakes you, creates cracks in your heart big enough for Satan's lies to filter through.

But this is when we fight back with wisdom from God's Word to recognize that the ability to tempt us is all the devil has. Beyond that, he has nothing—absolutely *nada*. And the truth, *muchacha*, is that you and I have everything we need through God's power that works in us.

So what are you waiting for? Pull back your shoulders and bring back that smile. Time to relish in the good news: You and I have the only weapon we need tucked in the compartment of our hearts— God's Truth. The truth that lifts us above the gloom, erases the negative thinking, and sizzles the enemy's lies to nothing.

With a new beginning, a new song of triumph, you can hold on to God's hand and savor the sweet truth that promises Jesus will get us out from under all that junk the enemy piled on us. Go ahead, dust off the dirt, straighten your hair, and put on your high heels of courage. Spray the perfume of boldness, and slip on the gold necklace of faith in God. We're ready for the final stop called "celebration."

And as we move forward, our steps are firm because we're equipped with weapons of reassurance. It doesn't matter what the doctors say; God has the final word. It doesn't matter what test results show; God's faithfulness prevails. No matter what bleak prognosis may come our way, God's purpose for our lives never changes. And it doesn't matter how hopeless a situation seems. God's power and might are working backstage to present victory in God's perfect timing.

Remember the woman who bled for years (Mark 5:25-34)? She knew all this. She was probably sick and tired of doctors' diagnoses that confirmed her illness but offered no possibility of a cure. And no doubt the enemy was whispering "There's no hope for you. God healed others but forgot about you. You'll bleed to death. You're case is hopeless." Until she brushed away her tears with the back of her hand, shook off lies from her heart, and in faith touched the hem of Jesus' robe. Then she was healed. The Bible says it happened instantly. But *muchachas,* the journey to that point was *muy, muy* long, and probably agonizing and draining.

And what if you're already on that journey toward healing, too—a journey that seems never-ending? Confused about God's silence, you are tempted to give up. The woman who touched Jesus' robe might have been tempted, too. But, just think. Maybe God's plans are already at work. God might be polishing your character, strengthening your faith, and gathering you close with great compassion and care.

I Told Him to Shut Up!

I've been there, *amigas*. And although it was a bit painful for me—humiliating, really—God chiseled at my character during those two weeks of waiting. Then, the day finally came when I would find out whether I had cancer. There I was at the doctor's office, wearing that silly thin robe with an opening in the front, my feet dangling as I sat on the paper-covered table and waited for the doctor to come in.

Then a crazy thought flashed through my mind. I remembered how I'd asked God to heal my physical eyes, but instead God did much more and gave me 20/20 spiritual sight. With that victory fresh in my mind, I inhaled a deep breath of reassurance. And before the doctor walked in, guarded against the enemy's lies, I became unusually proactive. I told the enemy to shut up.

Sí, I admit to being impolite. I don't usually speak that way to anyone. But assertiveness is a must when countering the devil's fierce attacks. I boldly bound his mouth, rebuked his destructive lies, and silenced his attempts. And you know how I did it? Like Jesus, I used Scripture. I repeated "Out of my way, Satan, because greater is he in me than you in the world. Be quiet with your lies for my future, because the Lord knows the plans he has for me. Plans to prosper me, not to harm me. Plans to give me a hope and a future. You have no power to cause fear in me because the Lord is the stronghold of my life. Whom shall I fear? Your craftiness cannot make me fearful or timid because the Lord has given me not a spirit of timidity, but of love, of power, and of a sound mind."

Remembering God's triumph, I inhaled deeply and lay very still while the doctor scanned the area in question. And I repeated to myself, "Should cancer be included in the findings, God had victory prepared for me way before I was born."

"No, nothing to worry about," the doctor said. "In fact, there's no need to biopsy."

What relief! After all the needless worry and struggles, and my hard-won victory over fear, I praised and rejoiced and cheered and called out a thousand "thank-yous" to the Lord.

But, *amiga*, your situation might be different. Maybe you *are* facing cancer, or you have been diagnosed with another chronic ailment, debilitating disorder, or terminal disease. Maybe doctors have given you but a few months before you nestle in Jesus' arms. If that's the case, let me share another story of how God has the last word, is in control, and guarantees the victory—even when doctors give a hopeless diagnosis. I'll let my friend Diane tell her own story—a story that proves God's power is as alive and active today as ever.

Diane's Story

I sat at the computer, trying to choose the right words for the kind of announcement I never imagined I'd be sending, even in my worst nightmares:

"Friends, I have some sad news. I was just diagnosed with a stage four of an incurable breast cancer. The doctors gave me four months. I refused any treatment, as doctors gave me very low odds of it helping my condition. I'm doing okay, accepting the inevitable. But rather than saying good-bye, I want to thank you all for being in my life. My days have been richer because of you. This is a difficult stage to endure, and one I never expected to travel. But life is unfair sometimes. Love and so much gratitude for you—Diane."

A few weeks before I wrote that email, a spider had bitten me on the breast while I was gardening. Concerned about the reaction, I visited the doctor. After a close examination, he said, "That spider bite is serious. But antibiotics will take care of it." He paused, and his expression grew somber. "It's not the bite that concerns us. But it's the red circle that formed on your breast."

The doctor ordered a biopsy, and when I came back for the results, he gave me the news. "It's not good, Mrs. Parker."

I leaned forward, my hands clammy. "What do you mean? All my mammograms and ultrasounds came back negative. I don't have any lumps, nothing at all." I choked as I asked, "You're not trying to tell me that I…" I couldn't even say the word.

"I'm afraid so. Diane, the biopsy, as you know, was quite involved because of the difficulty in finding the source. And it indicates with certainty you have cancer."

You have cancer.

Those three words blasted through my chest, a surge of fear paralyzed my body, and my mouth became dry. How could I tell my son, Tom? With me gone, he would have absolutely no one left.

"What kind of cancer?" I hoped my thoughts were running wild for no reason. Maybe the cancer was totally curable.

"I need to tell you, this kind of cancer is not only extremely rare, but aggressive, and so far resistant to chemo and radiation. We can try some treatment, but no promises. You need to understand."

He seemed to be suggesting the cancer was incurable. It couldn't be. This is the twenty-first century. Surely another specialist, a new treatment, or experimental drug could beat this disease.

My heart beat rapidly, and I gripped the arm of the chair. "What are the odds?"

"You have four months left."

Left? What does that mean? In four months, I'd be…I couldn't bring myself to accept that. I drove home in a daze, too numb to cry. But when I got home and told my son, my tears flowed with sobs I couldn't hold back.

His reaction was similar to mine—disbelief and sorrow. He had no family left but me. So, at every chance, he would snap pictures of me with his camera. He captured every moment—me in the house, me surrounded by flowers at EPCOT, me standing in front of various Disney attractions. He gathered them as if collecting gems for a future treasure chest.

I enjoyed his insistence on capturing our moments together. This was better than subjecting myself to senseless chemo treatments and harsh radiation with no real hope of a cure.

Over the next two months, I spent many sleepless nights trying to fit into the category of cancer victim. I hated that term and loathed that it was being applied to me. I needed strength to face this crisis, which at times seemed like a nightmare happening to someone else. I launched a prayer campaign. I requested prayers from contacts around the world—friends, acquaintances, co-workers, neighbors, church members, e-mail contacts, prayer ministries, clergy—all added to my own pleas before the Lord, all claiming God's healing.

During the day, strength came in spurts. I called an attorney to make arrangements, an unpleasant and painfully real task.

"And the house I'm building," I asked. "What will happen?"

"Don't worry. We'll get your deposit back and put it in the trust. Just sell everything you have."

The home of my dreams was put on hold, actually cancelled, along with all my plans for life. They all melted in the scorching heat of those three words: you have cancer.

Friends and family emailed and called often. "Think of this, Diane. You can do all the things you always wanted to do in these next four months."

That suggestion made sense, but in reality I had done most of what I wanted to do. Tom was grown; I'd traveled, worked, and lived a full life. I resigned myself to my fate, and with a strange sense of peace, I accepted the inevitable.

One morning, I received an unexpected phone call from my doctor. "Diane, we have some encouraging news." The excitement in his voice sent a warm surge of hope through me.

"Yes, what is it?"

"The results of the PET scan show the cancer has not metastasized as we expected. We found a treatment that we feel confident will bring better chances to defeat this type of cancer."

I held my breath. "What are the odds?"

"Eighty to twenty in your favor," he said.

Suddenly, God's hand became visible. And resignation turned to rekindled hope for a new beginning.

"I'm ready," I said.

"Well, it won't be easy." His voice turned somber. "It's the strongest and most powerful treatment we have. The side effects can be extremely difficult."

Difficult? Did he think for a minute I'd be scared of "difficult" when God was giving me a chance to live?

"Look, God is giving me one shot, and I insist on the most aggressive treatment available." I paused. "What do I have to lose?"

The surgery was scheduled for the following week. And I began to prepare myself for the "eight months of hell" the doctor said would follow. The strong drug, extremely deadly should it spill on any tissue other than the targeted area, had to be administered through a port. Strategically placed, it would pump the strong medication directly into my heart.

In the days leading up to the procedure, as I reflected on the coming ordeal, I began to doubt my decision to go through with it. The determination that had fueled me turned to discouragement. Why go through this? What if it doesn't work, and I only put myself and my son through more anguish? I was going to die someday anyway. I sobbed, aching with the temptation to give up. Then I realized I had entered a battle. God stood on one side nudging me to go on. And on the other side, my doubts reminded me of the chance this wouldn't work. But thanks to prayers from my friends, their friends, and folks I'd never met, I held on to the certainty that God would see me triumph.

"Go ahead," I told the builders. "Start building the house. I'll be busy and may not be able to supervise. But my neighbors will take care of anything during the process."

The builders began to hammer away, and my doctors continued the treatment process.

God provided medications and injections to decrease the side effects. The twenty-eight rounds of radiation and six chemo treatments weren't as devastating as the doctor had warned. My son Tom was by my side during each injection, each administration of drugs, each reaction, and each update from doctors. We both praised the Lord for positive results He would bring and looked for victory in all stages.

The radical mastectomy I endured described the change in my life—decisive and drastic.

"We removed sixteen lymph nodes," the surgeon informed my son after the surgery. "All sixteen had cancer. But although we believe we got it all, more chemo should follow."

Months of treatment would follow. But when the last session of treatment was over, the tests revealed no cancer cells present.

"What does that mean in the long run?" Tom asked.

"Your mom is technically cancer-free."

Praises to God flowed through my heart. My hope increased with each day. More tests and examinations proved all blood levels had returned to normal. My strength increased, my hair grew back, and sleep filled my nights. My color and skin tone returned to normal.

After I unpacked the last box in my brand new house, I hung a picture in my bedroom. It portrays a narrow path leading into a dense forest. Between the green tree leaves, bright sunrays shimmer through. The scene mirrors my life. "You have cancer." Those words threatened to defeat me. But instead, God had planned each stage and had prepared the outcome. And even when I couldn't see through the forest of shock, the Son shone the light of hope on me.

Listen UP!

Now you've heard Diane's story in her words. As of this writing, she has lived five years of cancer-free good health, and she seeks God's hand to give her another fifty.

Jesus knows the up and downs of our emotions as we enter the unfamiliar territory of disease. So he emphasizes: "In this world you will have trouble. But take heart! I have overcome the world" (John 16:33b).

Jesus said, "Take heart." *Amigas*, what he's really saying is, listen up, hear me out, and pay attention, *escucha*! So how can we doubt that he has the power to overcome and defeat cancer, blindness, mental illness, depression, chronic pain, or any human ailment? He reminds us: "I have told you these things, so that in me you may have peace" (John 16:33a).

With Satan's efforts defeated, you can face tomorrow with confidence because "The LORD will keep you from all harm—he will watch over your life; the LORD will watch over your coming and going both now and forevermore" (Psalm 121:7-8).

The Man and the *Sí*

Fear of loneliness clouds wisdom.

"Don't do it," I remember telling my friend Sandy. But I could tell by the look on her face that the charming man she'd been dating for just a short time had captured her heart.

"We love each other," she said with a dreamy sigh. "Besides, what's wrong with living together? We're engaged."

Even though I was no shy *chica* myself, especially during those college years, I knew sharing a bed with a man before saying "I do" in God's presence wasn't a good thing. But who was I to judge? And I was outnumbered in my position and scorned for my backward kind of thinking. My college friends said I was irrational in expecting a marriage certificate to make a difference. I was too young and lacked the influence to convince Sandy she was making a mistake. I tried to help her see other options, but she wrinkled her nose at me.

So she packed her things and moved in with him. Months later, he told her he wasn't sure he wanted to get married, didn't want to get tied down yet. My sweet, innocent friend did what any gal in love would do. She cried her eyes out because she'd given all of herself to him. Then she blamed him for his cruel betrayal and threatened to kick him out. Her dreams had flattened like flan without eggs. She sobbed her way to work each day, called me to complain about him, and repeated how much she loved him. And after the late-night shift of her part-time job, she snooped around, trying to find out if he was cheating on her.

What happened? The man she'd hoped would say, "I promise to love you forever," instead said, "I thought I loved you . . . but . . ."

I'll Be with You till the End

Those college days now seem like a lifetime ago. Over time, we all did grow up. But even though we now see ourselves as sophisticated *chicas*, we still dance to romance, only to find out the music isn't always pleasant, nor are the dance partners always charming.

"We're getting married," Maria, a lovely woman in our prayer group, shared.

We cheered, clapped, and asked the usual. "When's the date?"

"In a month."

A month? I thought that was pretty fast. But then I remembered she was fifty-five and he was in his sixties. Why wait?

Her voice bubbled with excitement. "I've had a prayer request tucked in my Bible asking the Lord to bring me the right man."

"So he's the one?" I asked.

"I think so. His wife died not long ago, and he contacted me. We actually go back a long way."

I decided to ask a nosy question. "Is he a Christian? A believer?"

"He said he attended a church years ago. I know he believes in God."

To this day, I chide myself for not pointing her to 2 Corinthians 6:14 to remind her of the importance of not being unevenly yoked. But I was a coward. Seeing her excitement, I couldn't bring myself to burst her bubble.

A few months into the marriage, my friend realized her *grande* mistake. Instead of exhibiting faith in God, her new husband faithfully catered to his adult sons—emotionally and financially. These two young men waged war against her. At every turn, they jabbed at her with rude attitudes and actions that actually made her break out in a rash. Her new husband did not defend her, nor did he show her any love or respect. Instead, he brought headaches and financial hardship into their marriage.

"But I thought he was the right one," she said through her tears. "I just wanted to have someone I could share the last years of my life with."

My dear friend is not the only one who hopped into a relationship with a man who whispered, "*Sí, sí*, I'll be devoted to you till the end," only to disappoint her.

I'll Love You if You Give Me What I Want

"I have to talk to you," Karen said to me on the phone. "Can I come over?"

Karen had a history of going through dramatic situations. Each had a logical solution. Logical in my view, that is, but not in hers.

"I hate myself," she said, slumping down on my couch. "I told myself I wouldn't do it. I was going to force myself to turn him down."

"What happened?" I said.

She sighed. "Well, he called me out of the blue and asked if he could come over after work and talk." She paused. "I said yes. I figured talking wouldn't hurt."

I frowned and chose my words carefully. "I thought you said you'd never see him again after what he did to you."

"I know, I know. But sometimes he can be a really nice guy. Besides, I was going to be strong this time."

The short version of this friend's story is that she fell for his "Wanna watch a movie in my apartment?"

You guessed it, *amiga*. The movie faded into nothing. And instead, without resistance on her part, his physical desires were met, and her self-respect slid away.

"And you know what happened afterward?" She paused to blow her nose. "He got a call, and I could tell it was another woman. Then he told me to leave his apartment. Just like that."

"What are you going to do?" I asked.

"Well," she choked with her sobs. "That's why I wanted to talk to you. I need your advice. He hasn't called me for a couple of weeks. I keep emailing him, sending text messages and voice mails. He never answers…so…do you think I should go and see him?"

My friend had sunk into the trap. She believed her man meant it when he said, "*Sí*, if you give me what I want, I'll love you." But he was lying.

How Can I Win Him Back?

Now it's my turn to join my friends in the romantic-failure department. Here's my story.

A few weeks after I had lost my sight, grief and bitterness filled my sleepless nights. You've already read about how God brought me out of that dungeon of gloom to the sunshine of divine love. But there was another piece of the story that I left out, dear *amiga*, because it fit better here where we're talking about romance, men, their lures and whims, and our crazy expectations from them.

When I was groping through life, blind as can be, my husband came home one night and said we needed to talk. He asked if I'd go for a drive with him. I held his hand so he could lead me out. We got in the car and drove in silence. Even after eight years of marriage and three kids, that silence made me uncomfortable, really uneasy.

"I…" Gene hesitated. "I don't think I can go on with our marriage."

I froze and then turned in his direction. Unable to see his expression, I held onto his words, hoping I could change them. "What's wrong?"

When he told me he had someone else in his life, every muscle in my body stiffened, my stomach cramped, and a lump blocked my throat.

"I...I need a bathroom." My words came out in a stutter.

He drove me to a fast-food restaurant, and in the ladies' room, I emptied all that was in me. But the blow, the hurt, and the rejection still seared my soul. The man I trusted, the man who had said "I do" before God, was now leaving me for someone else. My fate was clear: I would be divorced with three little boys and facing a world I couldn't even see. How could I stand it? All these years, I had counted on my husband. He had told me, "*Sí*, my loving wife, I'll provide for you, for all your needs and wants." But now he was preparing to leave.

So Where Did We Go Wrong?

Amigas, these stories are true. And maybe they sound all too familiar to you. Perhaps you've been through something similar. Well, I'm no psychologist or counselor, but I do know where to find good advice in situations like these. I will give you the plain, clear, yet powerful Word from God, who happens to be the best of the best counselors. The Lord charges nothing for advice, doesn't need to prescribe medications, and never makes mistakes with wise guidance. And the best thing is, God's counsel is available 24/7.

In fact, God was available for the woman at the well on that day, long ago. She had no way of knowing it, but the Lord had made that appointment even before she was born. We already talked (in chapter 2) about how Jesus set her free from her past. But let's take another look at her story, and see how gently he ushered her to the future. While sheep and goats were bleating in the distance, and the noon sun blistered on her head, Jesus began his session with her.

How strange that Jesus chose to talk with her about her relationships (John 4:16-18). He could have asked her about any topic. But he chose to talk about the men in her life. *Amigas*, could it be because Jesus knew which part of our lives often causes grief, sparks anxiety, and keeps us awake at night?

Of course, Jesus knew it then, just as he knows what you and I go through today. He's also very aware of how we try to cope with these situations and the emotions they cause. Some of us have mastered the cover-up routine. We go through life trying to look refined with our hair carefully styled, our jeans maybe a bit too tight for our liking, and high heels to match the outfit. And from our shoulder hangs a purse with everything in it— from diapers to aspirin. We look like we've got it all together. But inside we're a complicated bundle of whims, desires, longings, and emotional cravings. We're just like the woman at the well. The only difference is that she wore a long robe, while we wear jeans.

Amiga, let's put down our purses and, like the woman at the well, let's bring our jar filled with insecurities, unmet desires, rejections, loneliness or fear for the future, and let's have a chat with Jesus.

I'll go first. My jar is heavy, and I'm panting from its weight. Feeling the heat of my shortcomings, with sweat beads on my tanned forehead, I set my jar down, straighten my wrinkled blouse, and look in Jesus' direction. Being the bold *muchacha* that I am, I want answers.

"Tell me, Lord," I begin. "Why did you create us with that place in our hearts that begs for a man to fill it?" I ask Jesus about that, because I know some of us would do anything in this crazy world to hang on to a man. I did that very thing when I was consumed with dating during my college years. I was craving the attention, compliments, and companionship of a man to fill that empty place in my heart.

The same was true for my friend Sandy, who moved in with her honey, hoping happiness and marriage would follow. And it was true of my other friend, Karen, who strutted into that man's apartment, fell for his "you're looking good tonight," and gave herself to him in every way. She too was looking for the love of a man to fill the void in her heart. And there was Maria, who signed on the dotted line of the marriage certificate quicker than you could say "honeymoon," trusting that she'd found a man who would be the companion to fill the emptiness for the rest of her life.

And how about the *chica* with a physical abuser who torments her behind closed doors? Even before the welts heal, she drops the charges she pressed at the police station. And with dread in her soul, she goes back to him, risking further abuse and mistreatment of her kids.

"Lord, tell me please. What possesses us to walk down that path?"

What Man Is That?

I'm thinking back to another night, shortly after my husband told me he wanted to end our marriage. I was lying in bed, staring into the darkness, tears dribbling down the side of my face. My sons—ages three, six, and seven at the time—were asleep in their rooms. I was desperate, agonizing about my complete blindness. And to add to my anguish, hubby's side of the bed was empty. He wasn't home yet—he was with someone else. The pain and rejection stung right to my bones. How could I live with this open wound reminding me I was without the man who occupied the number one place in my life? The handsome man who just eight years ago had said, "I'll love you for better or for worse. For rich or poor. In sickness and in health…"

Those words meant nothing now. Instead of warm memories, the wedding ceremony was a cruel reminder of crumbled dreams.

I couldn't stop thinking of my fate. I chided myself for not being a better wife. For not trying harder to be attractive for him. For not catering to his needs more effectively. I blamed and punished myself emotionally until my tears drowned me in regret.

But that night, as I faced the torments of an abandoned wife, Jesus saw my plight. How did I know? Because in order to survive, during the day, I began to soak myself in God's Word through an audio Bible. Every chance I got, I listened to verses, insights, promises, instructions. I listened till my ears smoked. God's truth penetrated my very soul. That's how I knew the Lord was close enough to hear my softest whisper.

Chicas, I put aside my pride, and Jesus in his tender, gentle way gave me some answers. Not because he found me to be extra wise or cute, but because I was desperate. But, as is often the case, he began by asking me a question: Who is the man you think should fill that spot in your heart?

Being the quick *chica* that I am, I responded that it was my husband. The man I wanted to win back. He was the person I loved most. He was the man God had given to me as my partner for life.

Incorrecto! Wrong answer. Jesus was about to set me straight. He pointed to a well similar to the one where he and the woman had stood so long ago. I took a look. Yuck! In it I saw floating debris, especially my misconceptions about men. My misguided expectations that a man would satisfy my emotional needs. My misdirected hunger for a set of arms to make me feel secure at night. My misplaced trust that a man would be my provider. My distorted longing for a man's "*Sí*, I love you" that would seal his commitment to me for life. And my silly belief that a man would make me complete. All that was floating in the murky depths of the smelly well water in my Latina heart.

No wonder Jesus said, "Everyone who drinks this water will be thirsty again" (John 4:13). Thirsty…and with a bad case of spiritual indigestion, I might add. And we so often prove him right.

Year after year, relationship after relationship, we've been drinking of the water that cannot satisfy, and then wonder why our thirst is never quenched.

Chicas, here's where you need to sit up. Put down that cup of espresso. You're about to hear the solution we all need.

Jesus said, "But whoever drinks the water I give them will never thirst. Indeed, the water I give them will become in them a spring of water welling up to eternal life" (John 4:14-15).

Without a blink, I accepted his offer, began to take sips, and have never stopped. You might have too. And what a beautiful spring of water it is. Can you almost taste the sweet freshness? And we don't have to earn it. We don't have to pay for it or wait to get it. No "allow seven to ten days for delivery." It's ours the moment we hold out the jar of our heart for Jesus to fill it.

But the news gets even better: The clear water from Jesus that replaces the murky well isn't available just for a night or a season or even a lifetime, but for eternity.

He's the Man

That spring of water pours out what we need and what our souls thirst for—comfort, guidance, strength, and wisdom. Whether you flirt your days away, or share a bed with a not-your-husband kind of man. Whether you say, "Sí" to that good-looking male, who whispers soothing lies in your ear, or have a husband who said "I do" to you but "did" with someone else. Or if you can't find the courage and strength to say "no more" to physical abuse. Whatever our situation, Jesus knows what we need, and pours out for each of us a perfect portion from his oceans of wisdom.

Jesus knew what I needed, but I was clueless. I was too busy crying my nights away, hugging the pillow for false comfort. Who could blame me? *Mi esposo* had another honey, and I was alone and hurting. But in the morning when I gave one more sigh before I faced the day, God's Word filtered through. And the water Jesus offered gushed the wisdom to triumph over my sorry situation. We're talking about wisdom enough to recognize that God, with measured precision and intricate detail, crafted our heart. And the Lord purposefully carved out a specific spot uniquely identified as "only for Me."

Aha! That's why no human and flawed man can ever fill that spot. Only God can fill that spot. No one else could. No one else should.

I dare say that through the centuries, too many of us have made the same sorry mistake of trying to jam a flawed and weak man into that God-only place in our hearts. The result? An aching void, a hollow spot that still thirsts.

Smiling big at the new revelation, I took another sip of that clear, fresh water. And the taste of confidence was delicious. God gave me the confidence to face my husband's infidelity and resolve it with dignity and grace.

"We need to talk," I said to him when he came home late one night.

We sat in the family room, and I turned in his direction. "I didn't force you to marry me. And I won't force you to stay with me either."

My explanation wasn't prepared or planned. But my thoughts were clear and sincere. I poured out what I'd been drinking—the living water Jesus offered from his Word. Jesus had said he would be my provider. He would be the one to sustain me through lonely nights. He would be my companion when I felt abandoned. He would fill the void when I no longer had my husband's arms to hold me. And Jesus also promised he would fill my needs. The needs he knew I had even before I knew them myself.

Jesus also gave me his Word that his love would never end. He'd never walk away. And his Word could be trusted, because he'd proven his love for me on that rough, splintery cross.

"We both know the counseling sessions didn't help," I said. "And I don't want you to feel trapped. If you need to leave…" I took a breath. "You can go. The boys and I will be okay, because I also have someone else in my life. His name is Jesus."

Sí, amigas. I was more than a tad firm with my assertions and my positions. The reason is that I had left the "poor me" *chica* behind. I'd shed that silly approach that rode on my emotions. And I'd discarded the poor-me syndrome that left me sniffling into my wrinkled tissue and making a fool of myself. And I refused to paint a picture of a pitiful, sorry, clingy, miserable gal. Without pretense, pride, or self-righteousness, I clung to my secure stand because Jesus was by my side.

This is the same security Jesus wants for you too, his beloved, worth-dying-for *mujeres*. He never wanted us to stay in the "Cinder" part of Cinderella. Jesus died to make us his lovely daughters, worth receiving the best, purest, everlasting Love.

Not Yet, Buddy

A few weeks passed after that night when I displayed my convictions before my husband. Then one night, he came home and, once again, wanted to talk. He informed me that he had made his decision: He was choosing to end his other relationship, continue with our marriage, and renew his commitment to me and our sons.

The old me would have shot to my feet, hugged his neck, and planted a huge kiss under that prickly mustache. But the new me didn't. Instead, I lifted a palm in the air. "Not yet. If we're going to make it together, we need Jesus in our marriage. If we don't center everything on him, we'll never make it."

He agreed, and he also agreed to begin to pray together. In turn, I learned the importance of complete and genuine forgiveness. We fell in love all over again. And *chicas*, to my delight, Gene's transformation was so dramatic that sometimes I think he follows the *How to Be the Best Husband* manual he must have hidden under the mattress. In our thirty-five years of marriage, his tenderness, love, devotion, and commitment make my heart smile. But although his devotion is a crown in our marriage, Gene is still a runner-up. When it comes to occupying the *número uno* place in my life, Jesus is the one who fits perfectly in that spot of this *chica's* heart.

Although my story has a happy ending, I still wonder why I had to endure that painful episode in my marriage. Maybe it was so I could pen these words to you, *amiga,* so you won't fall into the well of romantic murk. So, instead, you might be nudged to rearrange your heart and make Jesus the man of your life. From firsthand experience, I can tell you that if you do, he'll fill your every need. Then human relationships will make sense. They will thrive with health and blossom.

And here's the bonus: behind closed doors, with candlelight shimmering in the corner, the love your *esposo* whispers to you will have a sweeter sound because you receive it with the confidence you drew from God's Word.

He Loves Me, He Loves Me Not

When we mess up, sometimes we ask ourselves, "What if?" What if I had done things differently? Gone a different path? Chosen another option? My friends Sandy, Karen, and Maria might be asking that very question. The happiness they sought was within reach, if only they'd accepted the water of wisdom Jesus offers. Had they filled their hearts with the spring of water welling up to eternity, their scenarios might have been so delightfully and drastically different.

Sandy would have looked right into the hungry eyes of her honey and said, "No, if you want to live with me, I expect commitment, respect, and devotion through marriage vows before God. And big boy, a bit of news here: God happens to be just a tad wiser than you and me." Besides, there's more to sex than skin on skin. Sex is as much a spiritual mystery as physical fact. As the Scriptures say, "The two become one." Since we want to become spiritually one with the Master, we must not pursue the kind of sex that avoids commitment. That will only leave us lonelier than ever because we can never "become one" (1 Corinthians 6:16-17, THE MESSAGE).

And how about Karen? Had she sipped a drink from God's Word, she may have had the strength not only to resist temptation but also to use God's wisdom to choose a man who saw her beyond her curvy legs. And rather than trying to prove his manhood in bed, the man she'd choose would prove his integrity and character instead.

And Maria who waited for decades for Mr. Right? Filled with God's wisdom, she would have the confidence to see the important qualities her Mr. Right lacked. She would know to avoid a marriage to someone who didn't share her beliefs and convictions. She'd see the red flags that warned her of the heartache ahead. And if God's plan is for her to spend her remaining days with the other side of the bed empty, the Lord would satisfy that craving for the warmth of a man. Not only that, but as Jesus did for my friend Nancy (whose story you read in chapter 2), her divine husband would fill her every day with overflowing contentment, fulfillment, and joy.

And how about the woman who stayed with the violent man and endured physical abuse over and over again? Had she tasted the water of security Jesus offers, she would have drawn courage to set boundaries. To seek help and draw strength to move forward. She'd stand on the truth that Jesus is her provider—financially, physically, and emotionally. And shedding fear, she would hear God's Word singing new reassurance to her: "I will answer them before they even call to me. While they are still talking about

82

their needs, I will go ahead and answer their prayers!" (Isaiah 65:24, NLT).

Now it's your turn, dear *chicas*. I invite you to pause for a moment and ask yourself: How have your relationships been? Does the man with his "*Sí*" still knock at the door of your heart? Or are you're still longing for that very knock that leaves you wanting night after lonely night?

I say it's time to do the wash. Let's rinse our hearts of those notions of what we thought we wanted, needed, yearned for, dreaded, or even feared. And with the fresh living water of Jesus' love saturating our hearts, begin again—clean, healthy, and prepared. Should a man come into your life, he'll see a different and unique *chica*, sparkling with an irresistible glow of wisdom, confidence, and grace.

7

Is That All There Is?

The fear that we don't have enough is
a poison that kills contentment.

My friend sat across the table in our favorite restaurant. "I hate you," she said with a grin. "Look at how much you eat. And you never gain weight."

I smiled while I took another forkful of my huge salad topped with a moist piece of salmon.

"It's not fair," she said. "All I have to do is *think* about a piece of chocolate cake, and my hips begin to grow."

I love my friend Rita. She has a refreshing way of telling me things. But she's been making that same comment for years. So one day, I responded, "Okay, let's make a deal. You give me your eyesight, and I'll give you my metabolism."

She laughed.

That interaction, as silly as it was, reflects what goes on in the heads of us *chicas*. We want what others have. I've done that, too, but more so at certain times of my life. All kinds of "wanting" swirled in my Latina head before Jesus tapped at my heart and I motioned him to come in. After I lost my sight, I was the queen of what the Bible calls "covetousness." And my wanting was in ridiculous areas. I was envious of friends who had the ability to shop for their own clothes, put on their own make-up, style their hair, read their mail, and hop in their car to head for the mall to catch the latest sale. I lamented my limitations and coveted what I couldn't do or have. Bitterness and anger flared up each time I thought about my life.

They Made Fun of Me

Although your "most wanted list" may be different from mine, coveting is the same on all levels. And this crazy kind of desire for what we don't have begins somewhere. Mine started way back in Bolivia.

Television was non-existent in the sixties in our hometown of La Paz, so we learned about the wonders of the United States through friends and acquaintances fortunate enough to have visited there. And like the suitcases they brought back packed with bargains from U.S. malls, their heads came back jam-packed with stories and descriptions of what they saw. We gasped with admiration at the details. Discontented with Bolivia's corrupt government and our country's lack of opportunities, we salivated for a new life in the United States. Like millions of others, my parents rolled up their sleeves and began the preparation to emigrate: gathering documents, certificates, and letters of reference, and depositing a large sum of money in a U.S. bank. The process took four years. Then one day we got the green light.

"Look!" My father dashed into our tiny, dark kitchen in La Paz, papers held up in the air. "The American consulate approved us."

That meant we'd finally be heading for Wonderland and moving next door to Alice.

Ha! No, *señor*, quite the opposite.

Once in America, we unpacked our suitcases while my *papi* praised the efficiency of the U.S. traffic police. They'd stopped us as we drove away from the airport. Papi thought the officer was conducting a routine car check. *Como?* How can that be? That wasn't a routine traffic check at all. We learned later that Papi had received a speeding ticket. *Sí*, that was the beginning of our adjustment period. Kind of sad.

First, we knew no English—a large setback at that time. No interpreters were available. No "press 2 for Spanish" options on any automated menu. We relied on a secondhand dictionary to make sense of those English words. And the results sometimes weren't pretty.

The journey began with my *mami* and *papi* tiptoeing into the workplace.

"I work free. You like, and you keep me. You no like, I go." Mami got those clumsy phrases from the limited English she knew. She managed to convince the *gringa* to hire her. But she didn't know the boss would sear her heart with harsh treatment. And that experience was the cross Mami carried during the years of her employment.

Papi came home from work downcast, and fatigue painted his brown face. His boss had shouted at him. "You idiot..." That's all Papi understood. The rest was garbled, unknown utterances in English. Later, he learned the reason for the chef's frustration. During the busiest time in the hotel's restaurant, Papi had been asked to order a case of lettuce. My *papi* had understood the "lettuce" part, so he had purchased one head of lettuce rather than a case.

My brother and I also struggled through the adjustment period. A note I brought from school detailed the attire for gym class. Mami paged through the dictionary searching the definition of "gym shorts." With the image of such a garment in her head, we headed to Sears. Weaving through racks of clothes, we were awed at the variety and abundance. We chose a pair, moderately priced with green and bright blue horizontal stripes. They fit fine, a bit snug around the legs, but they met the description in the dictionary.

When the rest of the sixth-grade girls removed their uniform skirts, I did too. The roar of giggles that filled the room pressed against me like bricks. They all wore navy blue tailored shorts. And me? I sported women's long underwear.

My brother didn't escape the humiliation either. On the way home from school, two kids from the neighborhood chased him and asked for his lunch money. He had no clue what they were saying, so they pushed him, punched him, and took his quarter. He didn't care, but I did.

Sometimes I scratch my head and wonder: Why did we stay? I have no idea. All I know was that we were in the land of confusion. We weren't content in Bolivia. But after arriving in the country of greatness, we weren't content here either. I was too young to figure it out.

What a Great Friend

What made our adjustment bearable was the new friend we met. He popped in on a regular basis. Mr. T was always full of stories and fun and was truly entertaining. We'd never known anyone like him. At first, we didn't understand much of what he said, but the more we listened, the more we learned. And pretty soon, my parents also slipped onto the couch beside us, mesmerized by his creative way of bringing fun into our cultural adjustment.

I remember one day Mr. T showed us a pretty green bottle with "Prell" written in big letters on it. The shampoo, he said, would make my hair shiny and beautiful, so I begged Mami to buy it. That began the cycle of wanting, of craving what we didn't have, and itching to get what we couldn't afford.

I know you're smart, dear *chicas*. You know how Mr. Television molds our thinking, and shapes our values. And you know how he (with the help of his cousin, Mrs. Media, and their friend, Holly Wood) can slither into our thinking, tainting our desires and installing a craving for gratification, making us believe it was contentment. How clever they are!

As we grew up, we went from wanting the cream to cure our acne to desiring the kind of coffee that would make our day better. We were hooked. A hunger for gratification became part of us. The more sophisticated the product, the deeper the satisfaction, they tacitly claimed.

Years came and went. We grew up. And once I was fully "Americanized," I joined the searching sisterhood. We're all members, aren't we? We're constantly searching for that something. We'd be happy if we had a different husband. A better job. And *sí, claro,* we would be satisfied if our kids were more successful. If we dropped some pounds. Peace would filter through if our health improved. Or if we finished the deck in the back or installed new kitchen cabinets.

The problem is that, even before the paint dries, we're hugging the pillow of discontentment because we're already planning to get the next thing on our list. Sad, isn't it?

That's because when we finally get any of the above, for a while, gratification makes our heart smile. But *caramba!* Contentment is still as elusive as beaches in La Paz. So, what's the answer? Are we supposed to let go of our search for contentment and settle in the couch of complacency?

Abuela Had the Recipe

She always did. But unlike Martha Stewart, Abuela followed recipes that were simple and required few ingredients. And when it came to her formula for life, she followed a similar simple method. She read the Bible. Often. And that's probably where she found two important insights: contentment is a way of life, and complacency is a cousin to laziness.

Dios mio! I wish I could have sipped Abuela's wisdom on *this* as I did her mint *té*. But, although a bit uncomfortable for me, I had to learn the not-so-good side of complacency.

You see, all pride aside, when it came to writing, I found that it came naturally to me. Naturally bad, that is. I used to wrinkle my nose at those bizarre grammar rules, punctuation, diction, syntax, sentence structure, and, heavens, that rule about avoiding those dangling participles. The only thing that dangled in my mind was a huge question mark about what that *loco* term meant.

But I had additional reasons why I was reluctant to take on the challenge of learning to write good (or is it "well"?). As someone who spoke English as her second language, this *chica* felt she had no business stringing words together and expecting they would resonate in the hearts of English-speaking readers. And I had one more excuse. Being blind, I had every logical reason to cross my arms and grin with relief that I was spared the effort. The only word I'd write would be "complacency" on my forehead.

But, *amigas*, in a secluded corner of my heart, I'd stored tons of episodes where God's hand had rescued me and set me free from gloom, despair, and grief. And that invisible way the Lord worked in my life bubbled up in me, wanting to spill over pages for others to read so that I could point them to Christ and nudge them toward finding the same hope that made me smile.

The options were clear: Obey God's prompting to write or decide to forget the effort, pamper myself, and sip *té* while listening to fun audio books. But I know that giving in to the latter would have made me discontent and restless. When God has a plan for us and we ignore the Spirit's call, dissatisfaction follows. That's why knowing the difference between what God has planned for us and what we want changes the channel on the television of life. When we hand over the remote control, God turns on a different program—one that follows God's plan even if it contradicts our whims, our comfort, and our complacent ways.

She Married a Fool

Complacency can have a variety of tough consequences. It does today as it did in biblical times. Look how Abigail's blend of sassiness and humility saved the day. The story of her non-complacency is told in 1 Samuel 25. She was married to a wealthy man named Nabal, whose name means, "fool." The Scriptures say Abigail "was an intelligent and beautiful woman, but her husband was surly and mean in his dealings" (1 Samuel 25:3).

Imagine that. A marriage similar to many relationships today. Some women marry bright, devoted men. And yet others say "I do" to men who don't exactly complement them, don't follow Christ, and don't bring much wisdom to the marriage. Nabal fit that description. He gave an idiotic response when he learned David's army had spared his men from danger. Rather than show gratitude, he questioned the messenger and scorned David's kind gesture. Have you known men like Nabal? They don't listen to reason. They're stubborn, and make life miserable for those around them. Nabal displayed his foolishness to everyone. And his reaction sparked fury in David, who drew his sword and ordered his men to attack Nabal and his men:

> Meanwhile, one of the young shepherds told Abigail, Nabal's wife, what had happened: "David sent messengers from the backcountry to salute our master, but he tore into them with insults. Yet these men treated us very well. They took nothing from us and didn't take advantage of us all the time we were in the fields. They formed a wall around us, protecting us day and night all the time we were out

tending the sheep. Do something quickly because big trouble is ahead for our master and all of us. Nobody can talk to him. He's impossible—a real brute!"

Abigail flew into action. She took two hundred loaves of bread, two skins of wine, five sheep dressed out and ready for cooking, a bushel of roasted grain, a hundred raisin cakes, and two hundred fig cakes, and she had it all loaded on donkeys. Then she said to her young servants, "Go ahead and pave the way for me. I'm right behind you." But she said nothing to her husband Nabal.

As she was riding her donkey, descending into a ravine, David and his men were descending from the other end, so they met there on the road. David had just said, "That sure was a waste, guarding everything this man had out in the wild so that nothing he had was lost—and now he rewards me with insults. A real slap in the face! May God do his worst to me if Nabal and every cur in his misbegotten brood isn't dead meat by morning!"

As soon as Abigail saw David, she got off her donkey and fell on her knees at his feet, her face to the ground in homage, saying, "My master, let me take the blame! Let me speak to you. Listen to what I have to say. Don't dwell on what that brute Nabal did. He acts out the meaning of his name: Nabal, Fool. Foolishness oozes from him." (1 Samuel 25:14-25, THE MESSAGE)

David did accept her apology and retreated from his attack. And later, after Nabal died, David made Abigail his wife

Wise and determined, Abigail had a choice. She could have sat before her wood-burning stove, and lamenting her fate, cried her eyes out. Or she could open the flap to her tent and toss complacency out. She chose the latter and took action. Fueled by the desire to save her people, she moved forth to do the right thing.

C'mon, *chicas*, if Abigail could do it, we can too. Time to say *adios* to complacency. We must, because if we don't, eventually we'll sink in the waters of anxiety. We all have areas that need to be corrected, changed or improved. What's yours? No matter what it is, you will find that inaction can be as dangerous as action. Being complacent can suck the joy out of us.

Often it's not laziness or idleness, but fear that presses us onto the complacency couch. God said it first: "God blesses those who work for peace, for they will be called the children of God" (Matthew 5:9, NLT). Sometimes our reluctance to "work" for peace keeps us tied to a difficult circumstance, suffering when we don't have to and enduring what we shouldn't. We find this tempting because we were taught as *niñas* that suffering is part of a woman's life. And, as our ancestors did, we are expected to submit to mistreatment. Because we want to be good *chicas,* we try to keep peace at all costs. The only problem is that there is no peace to keep. Instead, we find ourselves in the midst of a tornado of anxiety.

But God said to make peace. So it's up to you and me to get in the kitchen of life and prepare it. It requires large amounts of courage drawn from God's Word, portions of godly insight, many cups of patience, and all ingredients soaked in God's strength.

Moving On to Contentment

Complacency and contentment are as opposite as ballet and rumba. Complacency closes the door to peace; contentment opens it. But no one said it was easy. Seeking contentment, we may become *chicas* of action—eager to please, working hard, doing what's right, being a good wife, feeding the kids and the dog, smiling at hubby. But, *caramba!* Where's contentment? The answer came to me one night when I was counting my blessings. Suddenly

I realized my satisfaction was a bit incomplete. I just needed one more blessing, one more accomplishment, one more feather to brighten my *sombrero*.

Did you ever hear the story about when an outrageously wealthy man was asked how much more money he planned to have? He answered, "A little bit more." How insane, I thought. He has enough cash to buy New York, and he wants more? But really, *amigas*, we're all in that mode. We always think we want one more thing. And with new resolve and *mucho* passion, we set off to reach higher heights.

Now it's time for my confession. Here's my ambitious side exposed for all to see. Eventually, I moved beyond complacency and decided to write. *Bueno*! That part was good. But in the process, something subtle happened. I began to covet other writers' achievements. I hoped and wished for what they possessed: tons of literary awards and pages filled with Google links to their accomplishments. Dressed in envy green, I coveted that kind of success, imagining my book title and name on the best-selling list. And grinning with anticipation, I planned to embark on book-signing tours from sea to shining sea. My publicist would have to choose which interview request to accept first—*Oprah* or *Buenos Dias America*. And with the fat royalty checks that would pour in, I'd pay off our credit cards, and hubby and I would take off for a week in Hawaii.

Que tiene de malo? What's wrong with that dream? Isn't that the American way—to shoot for the moon? If we don't reach the moon, we'll still be among the stars. The problem is we set our goals ignoring the "EV" factor—eternal value—those things that hold worth for eternity. Without EV, when we reach the stars, we'll find it's hard to breathe, and our disappointment will be as big as the moon craters we were aiming for.

Remember Marilyn Monroe, the blonde movie star who was famous in the 1950s? She possessed it all—worldwide fame, beauty, money, and a future brighter than her smile. But with no "EV" guiding her life, she dipped into despair and tragically took her own life. And we know she's not the only one. Thousands of "successful" people have ended up either bankrupt, on drugs, or in a mess. Why is that?

Rick Warren, in his book *The Purpose Driven Life*, reminds us: "It's not about us, it's about God." How simple, clear, and direct, but how hard to live out—at least for this *chica*. I knew seeking worldly success was a losing game, but I still wanted to write the best book, the kind that would ignite a buzz so hot it'd give a face-lift to Facebook. And secretly, I expected my picture, shining with success and contentment, to be splashed on the homepage of my website.

Then the apostle Paul dampened my dream. In his bold, direct style he said:

> My counsel is this: Live freely, animated and motivated by God's Spirit. Then you won't feed the compulsions of selfishness. For there is a root of sinful self-interest in us that is at odds with a free spirit, just as the free spirit is incompatible with selfishness. These two ways of life are antithetical, so that you cannot live at times one way and at times another way according to how you feel on any given day. Why don't you choose to be led by the Spirit and so escape the erratic compulsions of a law-dominated existence? It is obvious what kind of life develops out of trying to get your own way all the time: repetitive, loveless, cheap sex; a stinking accumulation of mental and emotional garbage; frenzied and joyless grabs for happiness; trinket gods; magic-show religion; paranoid loneliness; cutthroat competition; all-consuming-yet-never-satisfied wants. (Galatians 5:16-21, THE MESSAGE)

Paul wrote this to the Christians in Galatia, but it's also for Christians in the United States, Bolivia, and everywhere else. And, thank goodness, he follows up his strong warning with a bit of encouragement:

> But what happens when we live God's way? He brings gifts into our lives, much the same way that fruit appears in an orchard—things like affection for others, exuberance about life, serenity. We develop a willingness to stick with things, a sense of compassion in the heart, and a conviction that a basic holiness permeates things and people. We find ourselves involved in loyal commitments, not needing to force our way in life, able to marshal and direct our energies wisely. (Galatians 5:22-23, THE MESSAGE)

Being the obedient *chica* that I try to be, I changed my thinking. Working to be a best-selling author is about me. But working hard to bring a message that points readers to Christ, that's about God.

Where to Find It

It's no wonder so many of us walk around frustrated, anxious, and stressed. We're looking for contentment in the wrong places. If we look for it in success, we'll find arrogance. If we look for it in relationships, we'll discover disappointment. And if we think contentment waits for us in a healthy bank account, we'll know emptiness.

The task ahead is different now. We kick off our high heels, slip on our Nikes, and get to work. The motivation has changed. Fueled by wisdom that helps us recognize tasks that fit into the EV mold, we give our all, do our best, and with God's seal of approval, gain the most. We gain the kind of contentment they don't advertise on TV.

Although the apostle Paul never met my *abuela*, he knew a secret recipe too, the same one you and I need to know. It's the best medicine for stress disorders and the flare up of fear. It's the cure that ushers in sweet happiness. But, *chicas*, the bizarre thing is that Paul learned this secret in an odd place—in a musty, dark, and gloomy prison. While there, he didn't rant, curse his fate, or rattle the bars in anger. Instead, he sang. *Sí*, he sang praises to the Lord. And probably with arthritic fingers, he penned words that have resonated through centuries: "I've learned by now to be quite content whatever my circumstances. I'm just as happy with little as with much, with much as with little. I've found the recipe for being happy whether full or hungry, hands full or hands empty. Whatever I have, wherever I am, I can make it through anything in the One who makes me who I am" (Philippians 4:11-13, THE MESSAGE).

Chicas, if Paul had to learn to be content, the learning applies to us too. Surely all those years we drank *café con leche* stirred our brain cells to learn without much effort. Time to get those *sombreros* out. We're heading into the sunshine of freedom. We're stepping out of the dark prisons of false security, of coveting what we shouldn't, of wanting what God hasn't offered us, and of longing for what lacks eternal value. Once we're outside, breathing in that freshness of freedom, we find contentment not at the end of the journey but on each step and at each stage.

The nosy part of me wants to know: *Y tu?* What stage of your journey are you on right now? Are you panting as you rush toward the finish line? Are you driven, with no time to rest, and have you forgotten there should be peace through the journey? When I ask those questions of myself, I realized the stage I'm on is called blindness. But rather than getting frantic and dashing around looking for treatments to restore just a little bit of eyesight, I found contentment in today's tasks, this moment's joys, this hour's challenges, and this week's God-given wisdom.

Amigas, the world is turning uglier by the minute. We hear about wars, face personal conflicts, live with disabilities, struggle with relationships that crumble, and stare at malnourished 401k accounts. And to top it all, the future mocks us with uncertainty.

We desperately want a change. We want all that junk to stop. And we so deeply want to be happy.

Queridas chicas, those changes won't happen. Because contentment isn't found in having what you want, but in wanting what you have. It's gratitude, genuine gratitude, that silences Mr. T and all the other voices that tempt us to desire more. As Jesus said, "You're blessed when you're content with just who you are—no more, no less. That's the moment you find yourselves proud owners of everything that can't be bought" (Matthew 5:5, THE MESSAGE).

At the end of the day, when the house is silent—our *esposo* and *niños* are asleep—we put on our soft slippers, slide into our comfy sofa, and ask ourselves: Right now, today, this moment, does my to-do list for life align with God's eternal purpose, or does it, instead, satisfy my personal preferences? Do the things I spend the most time, energy, and money on have eternal value—significance that will last beyond this world?

If the answer is *sí*, then from the depths of our soul and sincerity in our heart, we can whisper only for God's ears: "Lord, I'm in perfect, perfect peace, even if this is all there is."

8

The Melody of Hope Is Playing

If we fail to come to God,
we must fear healing will never come.

"I hate my life," I said as I took the tip of my pillow case and dabbed a few trickling tears. But where did the tears come from? I thought I had cried them all. "I don't think I can handle the heartache."

The house was painfully silent. And the nights were long and darker than ever. Only a few nights before, my nineteen-year-old son, Joe, had given me a peck on the cheek as he walked out the door for the evening. And now, he was gone forever.

Suddenly, I was shoved into the group of mothers with shattered hearts. With their worlds turned upside down, with unanswered questions, and facing days full of grief. I had expectations for Joe's future, but now they were thrown in the abyss of tragedy.

How do we moms go on when we must carry a burden that hangs like boulders from the heart?

Queridas amigas, before you think this chapter will bring you down, let me tell you something different: God will take us on the journey of hope, healing, and restoration. So go ahead, refill your bowl of tortillas and *queso* dip. Sit back, and together we'll watch God's way of restoring what tragedy had taken from us.

Did you know there are two kinds of people in this world? Those who have suffered a devastating tragedy and those who need to comfort them. Though I never would have chosen it, I fit into the first group. And with all that's in this Latina's heart, I will share with you how God took an unthinkable tragedy to a redeeming triumph.

We won't revisit the usual abstract insights. Instead, we'll visit the crevices of a broken heart. The shattered heart because of loss—of a child, a spouse, a parent, a friend. Or any other loss that covers your days with gloom—loss of health, independence, or anything dear—each of these can leave an aching scar. Together we'll weave through the agony, denial, anger, acceptance, and finally through the precious freedom from heartache.

It Came from Nowhere

When you wake up in the morning, no one ever says, "Excuse me, *Señora, Señorita,* let me make note of your preference for today. Would you like to break a fingernail? Or burn dinner? Or would you like to have a car accident? Lose your job? Or lose a child?" That's because all these things—big or small—catch us by surprise. We are never truly prepared when tragedy blasts into our lives. It is always cruelly unexpected. Sort of happy and a bit busy, we ride through life. We jot down our to-do list. We plan dinner with friends. Focused on the jammed schedule, we set dates and times to attend church meetings, kids' sports events, and social gatherings. And, being a pro at multi-tasking, we even surf the Internet to plan for bargain vacations in the sunshine state.

Then, without warning, the thunder of bad news roars, deafening and shocking. No more sunshine, appointments on the schedule, meetings, or plans. The blue skies turn black, lightning scorches our security, and the winds of pain flog us without mercy. And, *caramba!* The storm has just begun. Its destructive nature hurls us into panic. *Que pasó—y por qué?* What just happened—and why? The agony is real, but the reasons are elusive. The nightly news is blurting details that, before, were about other people.

About other victims. And now, to your anguish, they're about you. About your *familia*.

That's what happened to us. With a serenity that verged in coldness, the news reporter pronounced Joe's name as the victim. When I heard those details coming from our TV set, numbness kept me from lashing out. I listened with disbelief. Violent acts like this happen to other people, not to us—Christians who donate to Salvation Army and keep the lawn cut and weed-free. But that doesn't matter. The news spread like wildfire. Now, we were the people about whom the neighbors whispered. "What a shame...and they are such a nice *familia*."

Por qué? Why? The question echoes, sadly and futilely, because no one has the answer. But we still ask, believing that if there were an answer, it might help to lessen the pain or fill the void.

Then, a bizarre thing happens: We begin to think it wasn't real. It must have been a nightmare. And certainly daytime will erase the horrid details. But then one more person calls to say, "I'm so sorry about your loss. He was such a wonderful young man." Then reality strikes again. I did lose a part of me. My child is gone. I'll never feel his arms hug my neck again. My world has changed, and the reality is too huge for my mind to comprehend—much less, to accept.

No matter how we lose a child—a long illness, accident, or violence—the loss is still the same, the absence still as palpable. And because of that, preparation for a loss doesn't lessen the heartache.

Don't Make Me Go through These Steps

It all began one late night. *Mi esposo* and I had gone to bed, and the phone rang. Joe's brother answered, and then came to our bedroom. "Joe's been wounded."

My heart filled with fear. "Where is he?" I asked.

"Near here," he said. "They say to come right away."

My hands trembled, and my pulse drummed. We frantically grabbed clothes from the day before and dressed, then rushed to the place the caller had indicated. The paramedics and ambulance had already arrived.

"I want to go to him," I said.

"No, ma'am, you can't," one paramedic said. "We're working on him."

The ambulance took Joe away to the hospital, and we followed. As we waited and waited in that dark, cold emergency room, I repeated prayers, begging God to let my Joe be okay.

But then I heard the doctor's voice, "Are you the parents of Joe Eckles?"

I jumped to my feet. "Yes. How is he? When can we take him home?"

"Ma'am, I'm so sorry, but your son did not survive."

As the doctor related the horrifying details, my world turned blacker than ever. Joe had had a highway altercation with another man that ended up at a convenience store parking lot near our home. They both exited their vehicles, but Joe didn't know the other man was armed with a knife. My son did not survive the twenty-three stab wounds.

Ay, Dios mio! I was stunned and horrified as each detail emerged. I struggled to process what had happened. And the facts we reviewed over and over again didn't calm the storm. Instead, the senselessness of the act made it even more painful.

The days that followed were filled with funeral arrangements. How heart-wrenching and bizarre the preparations seemed. I was supposed to be preparing pleasant events—his college graduation, his next birthday party, or his next athletic achievement. Instead, *mi esposo* and I sat across the desk from the director at the funeral home.

"Here are the options," he said. "Which coffin would you like to choose?"

Which coffin would I like to choose? That question paralyzed my breathing.

"I don't know," I mumbled, my mind miles away.

"I understand," the man said.

But no one really understood. Choosing a coffin for your child is a task a mother should never have to undertake. Not for the little baby who grew before your eyes—the one you nurtured, made sure he ate his vegetables, and scolded when he disobeyed. His absence was a foreign thing. And so were the details—choosing songs for the service, choosing flowers, and wording the newspaper announcement.

I didn't ask for this. I didn't plan this—not now, not ever in my lifetime. I directed those complaints to the emptiness of my soul. Outwardly, I greeted all who showed up at the funeral, smiled at appropriate times, and masked my agony with words of gratitude. But when friends and family went home, fear pressed sorrow into my chest as I anticipated the coming days.

The Wrestling Match Began

When a tragedy of this magnitude explodes, the mountain of faith erupts like a volcano, spilling lava of doubt. *Sí*. Doubt. Questions, anxious questions. And to add to the mess, God's Word is diluted by our out-of-control emotions. Confused by pain, we dare to challenge their power.

"Be still and know that I am God" (Psalm 46:10). That verse burst into my heart the moment the doctor's news registered in my mind. But, unlike the clarity they'd held before, those words now didn't make sense. Being still wasn't what I wanted. I wanted answers, miracles. And I wanted all the bad news to go away. Besides, being still was impossible. My emotions were ricocheting off of everything. And my head was filled with dark thoughts.

That's when, dressed in sorrow, I entered into a wrestling match with God. God had promised to be "our refuge and strength, an ever-present help in trouble." (Psalm 46:1). "But if you were with me in that emergency room," I asked, "why didn't you hear my plea to save my Joe? Are you really as close as you say you are? Now I'm afraid, really afraid the aching void Joe left will never be filled."

"There's no need to fear, for I'm your God. I'll give you strength. I'll help you" (Isaiah 41:10, The Message).

"What about those moments when I'm about to fall apart, trying to face life's routine?"

"I'll hold you steady; keep a firm grip on you. Count on it" (Isaiah 41:11, The Message).

Ay caramba! There was no stopping me. With puffy, red eyes, I stomped my feet in anger. I countered God's promises with my pain, real and throbbing. Friends said this was a normal stage of mourning. Normal? For me, normal was Joe walking into the house, tossing the bag filled with his muddy football uniform in the laundry room, and giving me a hug with his muscle-bound arms. And while munching on the first thing he found in the fridge, blurting out witty comments. Even the silly ones made me laugh out loud. That was normal for me and my family. I resented the "mourning stages" or the "grieving process." They hadn't been in my plans as a mom to my three sons.

So on and on, the battle with God went on, round after round.

"Lord, when I see other families complete and happy, I tend to turn angry and want to lose my sanity. Will you hold me steady?"

"That's right. Because I, your God, have a firm grip on you, and I'm not letting go" (Isaiah 41:13-14, The Message).

"Over and over again, I try to understand why. Joe was only 19, so very young. Why did you have to take him so soon?"

"Trust God from the bottom of your heart; don't try to figure out everything on your own. Listen for God's voice in everything you do, everywhere you go; he's the one who will keep you on track" (Proverbs 3:5-6, The Message).

You'd think after a few weeks of this stubborn struggle, I'd let go of my rage and step onto the correct track. You'd think I would trust, settle in, and, with a humble heart, let God spread divine ointment on my wound. Oh no, not this *chica*. Still caught in the emotional turmoil that took place in the private quarters of my soul, God and I continued to wrestle.

Finally, fatigued from the struggle, I admitted the source of my complaints. They came from self-pity. For an unknown but bizarre reason, they gave me a distorted sense of comfort.

That's right. And to make it worse, the "poor me" syndrome blocked any notion of God's comfort.

It was time, *amigas*. Time for me to blow my nose once and for all, toss the tissue in the trash, and clear my ears to let God's words trickle again into my broken heart.

Dios mio! To accomplish that, I had to be as honest as David: "Search me, God, and know my heart; test me and know my anxious thoughts. See if there is any offensive way in me, and lead me in the way everlasting" (Psalm 139:23-24).

God didn't have to search too deeply. My fierce struggle, my waning faith, and my foolish anxiety-filled thoughts were all out in the open, exposed before God's eyes. And in the middle of all that, God saw the notion I'd hidden way deep inside: a Christian *chica* like me, truly devoted to Jesus and committed to following his ways, didn't deserve this punishment.

There it was: the naked revelation. I went from shock, to denial, to anger, to grief…and I was stuck there. The fact that I thought the episode was cruelly unfair and totally undeserved kept me from moving on to acceptance. And complicated *chicas* that we are, the opposite thinking is also true. In the midst of our pitiful sighs, some of us believe that because we've done something wrong or didn't love God enough, we're being punished. It's no wonder acceptance doesn't come; in our feeble minds, we turn the pain into an unmerited punishment.

Just How Long Will This Take?

I tried to be strong for my husband, whose grief was also evident. I felt helpless not knowing how to ease his heartache.

"I heard there's a support group for parents who lost a child," I said to him one night.

We decided to attend a session.

Friendly words and expressions of understanding buzzed through the large room. The attendees announced upcoming ceremonies in memory of their children. The person running the meeting gave details of upcoming events. And couples shared their stories. Joe had been gone for three weeks. Some of these parents had lost their children three years prior. But their pain still seemed raw. Their words choked out between sobs and angry tears. Who could blame them? No one can ever heal completely from such a loss.

Or can they? Can I?

On the way home I asked God how long this healing would take. "Do you plan to let me be like those mothers who, years later, still sob their days away?" That night I put the tissue box away. And with a hint of determination, I settled on the couch, slipped my headset on, and listened to the Bible. I stuffed thoughts of gloom in the drawer. And for the first time after long weeks, I had a clear head to pay close, really close, attention to God's voice through the verses of Scripture.

There, tucked in the Book of 2 Samuel was the answer: David, repented and restored in spite of his flaws and past sin, was called a man after God's own heart—a huge accolade for anyone. God loved this guy enough to make him king, great, powerful and charming.

But David's life wasn't always pretty. When his son became ill, "David prayed desperately to God for the little boy. He fasted, wouldn't go out, and slept on the floor. The elders in his family came in and tried to get him off the floor, but he wouldn't budge.

Nor could they get him to eat anything" (2 Samuel 12:16-17, THE MESSAGE).

I can almost feel the intensity of David's love for his son. Like him, we also enter the room of desperation and cry out to God for our loved ones.

> On the seventh day the child died. David's servants were afraid to tell him. They said, "What do we do now? While the child was living he wouldn't listen to a word we said. Now, with the child dead, if we speak to him there's no telling what he'll do."
>
> David noticed that the servants were whispering behind his back and realized that the boy must have died. He asked the servants, "Is the boy dead?"
>
> "Yes," they answered. "He's dead."
>
> David got up from the floor, washed his face and combed his hair, put on a fresh change of clothes, then went into the sanctuary and worshiped. Then he came home and asked for something to eat. They set it before him and he ate. His servants asked him, "What's going on with you? While the child was alive you fasted and wept and stayed up all night. Now that he's dead, you get up and eat."
>
> "While the child was alive," he said, "I fasted and wept, thinking God might have mercy on me and the child would live. But now that he's dead, why fast? Can I bring him back now? I can go to him, but he can't come to me."
> (2 Samuel 12:18-23, THE MESSAGE)

Honestly, *amigas*, would you do that? The minute you learn your precious child is gone, would you slip into your new outfit, curl your hair, put on some lipstick, and say, "I'm cool"?

No way. But here's the thing: David knew something so profound and true that made him react in an odd way—odd for us here on this side of history. He was making himself presentable. After his bath, maybe he put on a new robe not because he was headed to work or to war, but because he was going to the place of worship. And while in God's presence, David's heart had spiritual surgery—some of God's best work. The Lord carved the misconceptions right out of David's heart and poured in the sweetest, most profound and life-giving truth—that David would, indeed, see his son again. Imagine that! No wonder his appetite came back. Wouldn't yours?

Goodness gracious, *amigas*, let's think about that. It is a wonderful promise. But in my feeble Latina head, I had to ask: How in the world was God going to allow David to go and see his son again? Or allow me to see my Joe? And how would God allow you to see your loved one again?

Don't, for a minute, feel bad if this promise is a tad tough to grasp. If Martha struggled a bit, we will too. Remember her? She was the busy *chica* who prepared lunch for the Lord Jesus. And like us today, she probably had bangs stuck to her forehead from sweat, and flour on her nose. Maybe she even had a few stains on her apron. She complained and ranted about her sister, Mary, who was soaking in the freshness of Jesus' teachings instead of helping with the housework. But Martha, not happy about this, with fist on hip, huffed her way back in the kitchen.

I identify with this Martha. I was in the kitchen of mourning, ranting about my heartache. And in the process, I was sweating sorrow, and, on the apron of my soul, I had stains of bitterness for my loss. Martha missed the good stuff—the truth that had nothing to do with chores but everything to do with God's choice to send Jesus.

Later, after Martha's brother Lazarus died, Scripture says Jesus wept (John 11:35). The Bible doesn't say why, but I have an idea. I think he cried first because he had compassion for the suffering of the Marys and Marthas of the world. But I think he also cried because Martha, like me and millions of others, misunderstood death. Consider the conversation Jesus has with Martha when he first arrives at the tomb of Lazarus:

"Martha said, 'Master, if you'd been here, my brother wouldn't have died. Even now, I know that whatever you ask God he will give you.'" (John 11:21-22, THE MESSAGE).

I knew that, too. I had asked Jesus to keep harm from Joe. And Jesus could have done so if he wanted. But he didn't. So like Martha, I had questioned him.

"Jesus said, 'Your brother will be raised up.'

"Martha replied, 'I know that he will be raised up in the resurrection at the end of time'" (John 11:23-24, THE MESSAGE).

I knew that, too. Two years before Joe left me, he had attended a Fellowship of Christian Athletes camp. And when they explained the plan of salvation—how to guarantee entrance into heaven—Joe had invited Jesus into his heart. Eternity in heaven was promised to him. But I still wanted him with me, rather than wait for that final resurrection day.

What Jesus tells Mary next is astonishing: "You don't have to wait for the End. I am the Resurrection and Life. The one who believes in me, even though he or she dies, will live. And everyone who lives believing in me does not ultimately die at all. Do you believe this?" (John 11:25-26, THE MESSAGE).

Doesn't die at all? Those words resonated within me. I savored them like *abuela's* delicious *arroz con leche*. I repeated them again and again. Inhaling a huge breath of relief, I realized that I had to choose: Do I believe, truly believe? Or do I still doubt, dismissing God's Word and choosing to spend endless hours in mourning? Not because I'm smart or clever, but because I was sick of the distress diet, I chose the former. I changed my mind.

That's when, like coffee grounds, my dark, negative emotions settled at the bottom of my torn heart, counting on God's divine mending. I packed my bag of faith and tossed doubt out. I reserved a seat in the limousine and headed down the highway of healing. I brushed my hair, managed a smile, and found that my eyes didn't burn as much, because I rejected those self-pity moments. I got comfy on the seat.

While moving forward, I have found that sometimes, the road has large bumps. They're called birthdays, Christmas, Thanksgivings, and any time I feel Joe's absence more keenly. Moments when we remember our loved one's gestures, words, hugs, and kisses. Those bumps aren't all bad. If they jostle us, that means we're moving ahead. And we're not broken down on the side of the road of grief.

But be warned. The road also has potholes big enough for us to fall into. And when we least expect it, we can get stuck in the mud of lies. The biggest one repeats that we're separated from our loved ones forever. But if those loved ones knew Jesus and they began anew with him, great news: Even as you read this, your loved ones are busy choosing the perfect outfit to attend the reunion of all reunions.

And *que bueno!* The road also has rest areas where we can refuel our compassion. And with a good amount of this trait, we help others exit the house of heartache. With a smile of empathy, we scoot over, making room for them on the seat beside us so they too can ride the highway to healing.

The Accommodations Are Deluxe

Being physically blind, I spend much of my time imagining. In fact, I use my imagination every waking moment. Sometimes it works overtime. And when I try to picture my Joe walking on streets of gold, it's a bit tough to paint that scenery in my head. That might be because on this earth, we walk on the concrete of hardship, insecurity, and restlessness. We cannot imagine how it must be to reside in a place where the splendor cannot be explained nor divine details described. Not when sin, violence, and evil echoes from all sides. But this should be no surprise: "It was sin that made death so frightening and guilt that gave sin its leverage, its destructive power. But now in a single victorious stroke of Life, all three—sin, guilt, death—are gone, the gift of our Master, Jesus Christ. Thank God!" (1 Corinthians 15:54-57, THE MESSAGE).

Death, along with guilt and sin, is gone. Those we love are indeed walking on streets of gold.

> Can you imagine stepping on shore and finding it Heaven?
> Can you imagine touching a hand and finding it God's?
> Can you imagine breathing new air and finding it celestial?
> Can you imagine waking in glory and finding it home?[1]

No wonder Jesus wept. Maybe because he knew we missed the message? Maybe we overlooked the splendor prepared for us? We see death as the end. Jesus sees the new beginning. We dread its coming. He delights in its defeat. We think of it as a tragedy. He sees it as triumph already won. We fear its finality. He opens the heavenly door. We sink in sorrow. He lifts us up to life eternal.

Let's toss all that misunderstanding about death in the garbage disposal of confusion. And no matter who went ahead of you to God's house of glory, the healing is spiritual, the calmness is emotional, and the tender memories are physical. That's the beautiful balance that brings triumph to tragedy.

Mary and Martha learned this. When Lazarus's laughter stopped, he died and his sisters buried him. But Jesus raised him back to life to prove God's power at work through him. And the reason he didn't rush to do it was to prove he had control of the timing (John 11:5-6).

God's perfect timing—often contrary to ours, but perfect still. Joe's laughter also stopped. And, with a calm heart and a quiet soul, I accept the pause. *Sigo esperando*, I continue to wait. I'll be with him again. That anticipation is so very sweet. On that day, with my physical eyes, I'll see the sparkle in his hazel eyes and the warmth of his smile. Boldly secure, I gave myself permission to count on that fact. To believe otherwise would be to deny that Jesus, with one immense sword of love, killed death.

Amigas, it's time for you to place your sack of sorrow into Jesus' hands. He can handle yours. He can handle mine. And together we'll wake up to a new beginning where the mourning ends, the peace nourishes, the laughter revives, joy sustains, and security for the future strengthens. And after this earthly life, rather than an end, more life, endless and certain. The mariachi band plays again with *esperanza*—hope and expectation.

NOTE
1. As found on a plaque in a friend's home. Adapted from lyrics from "Finally Home," music by Don Wyrtzen, lyrics by Don Wyrtzen and L. E. Singer. Copyright © 1971 New Spring, a division of Brentwood-Benson Music Publishing (ASCAP). All rights reserved.

Finally, All Is Well with My Soul

*When we're wronged, acceptance is good,
endurance is better, forgiveness is best.*

"*Ay caramba!* How dare they do this to me?" We stomp
our feet and, with gritted teeth, wonder if God is listening
to our pain.

Amigas, let's be really honest. When wounded, we hate the
unfairness of life. And we want answers, solutions, and healing.
And we want them pronto, microwave style—quick and easy. But
reality mocks us. When we encounter betrayal, abuse, or deceit,
our world turns dark, and anguish controls our emotions. Initially,
como víctimas, as the victims, we're stunned, wounded, and dev-
astated. We can't even imagine recovering emotionally from our
complicated situations.

So we go through HELL. You read it right. But before you think
I'm being disrespectful, take a few bites of your *arroz con leche*
because we won't tiptoe through this issue. Rather, we'll be more
than a tad bold as we explore the junk that lines our hearts with
pain. You know we won't deal with superficial fluff. Here's what
HELL stands for:

      Harboring our hostility
      Embracing our pain
      Looking for an apology
      Longing for vengeance and lamenting our fate

Without a hint of pride, I admit I've walked on the hot coals of HELL. Maybe you have, too. That's why I invite you to join me and together we'll trudge to the place where we find the solution, the way out of HELL, and enter the heaven of freedom.

Harboring Our Hostility

Casi siempre. Almost always these elements of HELL describe the scenes that play on the stage of our wounded heart. We scoot out of the way of our rationale, logic, and judgment. *Muy bién*, good, now there's room for the hostility that burns inside. Who could blame us? Our reactions as *buenas muchachas*, undeserving and innocent, have the right to play hostess to bitter feelings. And *por qué no*? Why not? A degree of anger is to be expected.

Should someone offer counsel, we nod our head in agreement. But *adentro*, deep inside we want to say, "You're not taking my right to feel angry about this wrong. Not a chance."

Aún más, and another thing, the command in Ephesians not to go to bed angry? *No creo*, I don't think so. Surely Dios expected anger to fizzle out when our head hit the pillow at night only when facing lesser infractions such as someone cutting us off on the road, or when our *esposo* forgets our anniversary.

But when your life was turned upside down with a travesty no one should have to endure, all rules go out the window. *Seguro*, for certain, anger settles in the guest room of our heart. And without hesitation, we prepare hefty meals to feed and keep it alive.

Embracing the Pain

The degree of wrong you tasted doesn't matter. *Todas*, we all have this in common: At one time or another, we fall into that HELLish trap. We suffer betrayal; we burn with shock. We suffer disappointment; we linger in resentment. When someone wounds us, we bask in self-pity. And if someone mentions forgiveness, we run, shaking our heads vehemently. The notion of forgiving someone who has hurt us tastes like the cod liver oil our *abuelas* tried to force into our mouths. That's the problem—when faced with devastating pain, forgiveness seems out of the question. And sometimes the people who are toughest to forgive are those we have loved and trusted. The wounds burn raw.

"I can't stand it anymore," the letter said. It described an all-too familiar story—a spouse who committed infidelity. And with whom? With none other than a close friend.

They dragged their confused, shook-up emotions into the counselor's office.

"I can forgive" was the promise.

But even years later, confession came. "It still haunts me. I love my kids, and I want our family to stay together. But I can't let go, I can't release the hurt...."

Dios mio. Who could blame this wounded heart? When a spouse turns to someone else, the devastation is more than we can take. When my husband, Gene, confessed this very thing, my disbelief turned to anger and then anger became self-pity. I don't deserve this. I was the *buena esposa*, I thought, faithful, devoted—and I even attended his boring softball games. How dare he?

Oh, yes, those thoughts can stick like lizards on the screen around our swimming pool. Even when we think we've peeled them off, the nagging reminder we are sorry victims of infidelity slithers closer to us. And in futility, we try to forget and *sort of* forgive. Even intimate moments are tainted with notions of disbelief. *Nada, nada* seems like before.

Then the zany questions surface. What if *mi esposo* is tempted again? Will I ever really trust my partner? How can I make sure this never happens again? No matter how many "I'm sorry I hurt you" and "I promise I'll never do this again" expressions fill our make-up moments, doubt and suspicion kindle the flame of our own HELL. And secretly, we embrace the pain. *Por qué?* Why? Because that's our way to keep the hurt alive. If it's alive, then our spouse will never forget the horror of the betrayal, and will surely refrain from repeating it.

Incorrecto. Embracing the pain so tightly only weakens our arms. They're too frail to receive the peace and security only forgiveness brings.

Looking for an Apology

The marital bedroom isn't the only place where HELL takes residency.

"My dad wants to come and stay with us for a few days," a friend confided in me.

"What do you think you'll do?" I said.

"After what he's done to me? After all the years that have passed, I thought I'd resolved those feelings." She sighed. "But now with my little girls, things are different. I have to protect them. I can't forget what he's done. Not that I want to get even, but he has to pay." She paused. "Do you know he never even acknowledged it?"

Sexual abuse, no matter when it happens, how it happens, or who knew the details, leaves scars that never go away. Psychologists agree that a violation of this magnitude mars every aspect of one's life. The aching goes deep, and the struggle to heal can be even more profound when there's another person to blame, someone who knew about the abuse but did nothing to prevent it.

I'm no psychologist, just a sincere *chica* who observes the sorrow these women host. From what they tell, having the abuser face punishment or having him ask forgiveness might help the healing.

Often, *toda una vida*, a lifetime passes by and no apology is offered, no regret or remorse is expressed. And the heartache still throbs. It's constant and deep. *Que pena*, how very sad. And as they look for an apology that never comes, the sorrow flames the rage in their own HELL.

Longing for Vengeance, Lamenting Our Pain

"Yes, that's what he said to me. I will never forget his words."

Words are powerful weapons. And if they're cutting, like machetes, they divide families, chopping away any love between them.

"My sister won't go to our relative's funeral," my friend said. "She refuses because her son will be there."

I was stunned. What could possibly cause a *madre* and her *hijo* not to speak to each other and avoid their presence for more than twenty years?

This *chica* wouldn't dare explore the reasons. *No hay duda*, no doubt, each party has good reasons. Each person holds on to his or her ground, to his or her own logic and pain. And avoiding one another's presence is an effort to play out a secret desire for a bit of punishment and lots of vengeance. Ever so sadly, *sutilmente*, subtly, the HELL lingers, burning days away till they end on this earth.

"I won't rest until they pay," the mourning mother said to me when she called, looking for comfort. "The police have to pay for their negligence and for letting my child die."

I tried to comfort her. I did my best to make her see she should let go. But this woman clung to what she called her "mission in life." In her sorrow, she was blinded to the world's weapons to hurt. And she had closed her eyes to God's way to heal. Instead of satisfaction and peace, her passion to seek vengeance will probably add to her sorrow and put her too in the victim category.

The same HELL burns when we punish ourselves for something we've done or failed to do. The mistakes we made. The temptation we succumbed to. The heartache we caused or the harm we inflicted. The nagging guilt whispers to us, "You need to pay, *mucho*, in a big way." But...*hasta cuando*? How long? With sleepless nights, we wonder if the misery and self-emotional flogging have an expiration date.

"She's in counseling." I heard a friend relate the same story time and time again. The toddler's mom had accidently left a plumbing cleaner container on a low shelf. The little one placed the lid in her mouth and profusely burned her lips and tongue. After several plastic surgeries to repair the child's disfigurement, the mom's HELL continued to taunt her. The lingering guilt and self-blaming fueled her heartache.

As parents, we can blame ourselves more quickly than we can detect a dirty diaper. And as we've done umpteen times, we can discard the stinky mess. But tossing out guilt is *muy difícil*, far more difficult. So, we lament our stupidity, our senseless actions and our carelessness. We confess, we cry, we call ourselves names for doing whatever it was. And *pronto*, pretty soon, all rub guilt into us till it hurts. Forgiving ourselves just doesn't seem right.

So Where Is the Door to Exit HELL?

As you might expect, my *queridas amigas*, I have experienced a few of the above scenarios. My HELL was sparked by an unfairness. I'm not talking about the kind when your boss passes you by for a promotion. I'm talking about cruel, incredibly shocking injustice.

A year after our Joe was killed, the man responsible was brought to trial. The trial took *tres días*—the most difficult three days of my life.

Surrounded by family and friends, I sat on that hard wooden bench in the courtroom and listened to the details of my Joe's struggle on that awful night. While the medical examiner described each time the knife entered Joe's body, I felt as if the wounds were piercing my own heart. They seared right to my soul. Silently, I asked God for courage, for strength to endure this court trial. Finally, at the end of the third day, the judge read the jury his instructions. They asked us to leave the courtroom, and we waited outside.

Tres horas later the jury reached the decision. The bailiff opened the door of the courtroom. "The session will begin. All parties may enter." We filed in the courtroom in *silencio*. I gripped Gene's hand and the bailiff asked all to stand.

My heart throbbed. I pleaded with God. *Señor, we need to see justice.* The man had suffered only a scratch to his cheek and a bloody nose. He had to be punished for what he did to my Joe. *Señor, we need justice.*

The jury foreman took his place in front and read the verdict: "We find the defendant not guilty on all counts."

Not guilty.

Those words made me tremble.

The man had pled self-defense and was acquitted. Our side of the courtroom crumbled under that decision. The other side cheered.

Dragging our shattered hearts home, I cried out to the Lord: "*Dios mio!* How could you let such injustice take place?" I questioned God's sovereignty, faithfulness, and justice.

"Lord," I cried out, "you say we should know that you cause everything to work together for the good of those who love you and are called according to your purpose" (Romans 8:28).

But...*como?* How could this horrible injustice be turned to good?

Empty of answers, my HELL began.

I nurtured my feelings of loss and abandonment by the One who promised to be my defender and my refuge. I harbored hostility. Seated on the self-pity chair, I embraced my disappointment and pain. I had longed for vengeance through a stiff prison sentence, and I looked for an apologetic, remorseful offer from the man. And with tearful eyes, I lamented my fate as a victim of injustice.

Days dragged by, and nights never seemed to end. And all the while I tossed around reasons for why this happened to us

So When Does It End?

Each of the stories I've shared in this chapter, including my own, illustrate how we *chicas* can find ourselves roaming around in the dark basement of HELL where we really don't belong.

But, *una noche*, one night, glorious and sweet, I found freedom.

Gene and I had knelt together in prayer. Although it had only been a few weeks, we had agonized over that jury decision way too long. And with shattered hearts, we continued to pray. We prayed for strength. We asked God for healing and a relief from the sting of injustice.

"You know what we've not done," Gene said.

I thought we'd done all. Cried enough. Prayed enough. And we desperately sought answers often enough.

"If this man repented and was forgiven," he said, "he would someday be in heaven with our Joe, worshipping God." He took a deep breath. "We have to forgive him."

I sighed inwardly, feeling a bit guilty for not mentioning that myself. But the truth was that although forgiveness was an order from God, I needed time—to nurture my pain before taking that most difficult step. Forgiving him—didn't that mean I had to accept his crime and the injustice that followed?

I held my breath while the thought swirled in my head. Though not simple, the choice was clear. Refusing to forgive would put another lock on our prison of resentment.

"That's what we need to do." I agreed.

That night the doors to freedom opened. The prison that had

enclosed us with bars of heartache and anger crumbled. Forgiving the man didn't mean we would hop in the car, head to his residence, knock on the door, and with a big *abrazo*, offer our forgiveness.

But forgiving him *did* mean we had to rise above the HELL that had scorched our days. Although the man hadn't asked for our forgiveness, extending that grace of complete and genuine forgiveness was the gift we gave ourselves.

Rise Above?

Years have passed since we made that decision. And, *amigas*, based on that experience, I want to share a truth that might rattle you a bit: forgiveness isn't about what we feel inside. It's all about how we honor God above.

But is forgiveness even possible? *Sí*. But there's a process. First, we need to admit this world is grossly imperfect. Evil abounds. Dark times are inevitable. They happen, they hurt us, and they violate all we thought was sacred.

Second, it's *tonto*, dumb to ignore the stages of sadness, grief or hurt. But it's dangerous to dwell in these stages, to make a home in them.

Eventually, we must accept these events as part of life. Not in a robotic kind of way, but with a mature and sound mind that embraces serenity enough to take us across the forgiveness threshold. That's what I'd had to do years earlier, when we faced the infidelity episode in our marriage. I chose to step through the doorway into forgiveness. I forgave Gene *completamente*. No looking back. No holding that episode over his head—or in my heart. Each time I write about it, Gene approves and shares the passion to help other couples with the illustration of our victory.

In all areas of life, unfairness abounds. And justice may be blind. But injustice allows us to discover the beauty of forgiveness.

Beauty, in forgiveness? *Sí*. It's beautiful when we realize this wisdom from God's Word. Wisdom to know God expects forgiveness. Wisdom to accept that we can't undo the past. Wisdom to know that we cannot force remorse into someone else's heart, nor can we change another person's behavior.

Don't Ask Me to Change

Don't you hate it when someone says you need to do something but doesn't tell you how to do it? I'll be *diferente*. I'll spill the details. I'll show you how. *Amigas*, here is the turning point. *Por favor, escucha*. Sit up in your chair and listen. This is important stuff.

We can choose freedom. But it will cost us. We need to do something totally and completely contrary to our Latina way of doing things. We need to change our thinking.

Sí, you read that right. The change doesn't have to take place in the other person's heart, but in our own. To prepare *pollo con arroz*, the chicken has to be cooked. The impurities must be boiled out so we can avoid salmonella poisoning. That's the same with you and me. We need to let God boil away the notion that it's about our emotional fragility. That way, the Holy Spirit can remove the poison of embittered sorrow. When we focus on ourselves, *caramba!* We disregard God and the biblical mandate to forgive. And probably to God's divine chagrin, we dismiss the divine plan, the perfect plan to triumph and healing.

Jesus says, "If you forgive those who sin against you, your heavenly Father will forgive you. But if you refuse to forgive others, your Father will not forgive your sins" (Matthew 6:14, NLT). Did Jesus say, "*if you refuse?*" *Dios mio*. He must know us *muy bién pero muy bién*, very Very well. He knows our stubborn heart.

So *amigas*, the instruction is clear. It's time for that needed change. The change begins with the forgiveness you and I already received. *Sí.* Remember when we planted *flores* in the garden? Our hands got dirty, muddy and soiled. *Con mucha agua*, we washed them and scrubbed them. Without exception, all of us dug into the dirt of sin. But what did God do? Not condemn us. Not grin as we sizzled in our sin in preparation for eternal hell. Instead, Jesus ran the water to rinse us from sin. Are you ready? *El nos perdonó*, he forgave us, through and through. *Gracias, Señor Christos*!

I've Got My Rocks Ready

In John's Gospel, Jesus paints a chilling scene. It begins in an awful setting. A woman is brought before Jesus who's been caught in the act of adultery. The Bible doesn't give further details, but she probably snuck into a steamy tent or dark room. There she snuggled with someone to whom she wasn't married. This was more than a bad-hair day for her because she got caught. She was dragged to a rock fest for punishment. The scene wasn't pretty, and she must have known what awaited her. Don't you wonder what went through her head? *Seguro,* she was regretting the time she'd spent with that man. He definitely wasn't worth the rocks that were about to shower down on her. He was guilty too, but was he willing to share the consequences? No, she was alone before her judges. We're talking injustice bigger than the blue skies above.

Chica, maybe you've walked a similar path. You plunged into a relationship that, like a bad movie, was kind of exciting in the beginning, a little interesting in the middle, but then, *que pasó?* The end stunk. While the unpleasant smell lingered, you didn't know how to undo what happened. *Gracias, Señor!* Thank you, Lord, at least in Western culture, our sexual indiscretions aren't punishable by stoning. If they were, we'd have a serious rock shortage.

In our Latina culture as many others, like changing hair styles, we've seen shifts in values and attitudes. But God's truth hasn't changed. And although the Lord offers forgiveness at every turn, the ugly consequences of our sin strike *dia y noche*. They may be the rocks of regret that pelt our hearts, or stumbling stones of shame that trip us when we try to move on, or huge boulders that obstruct our forward progress. All block us when we encounter aching memories of one moment of pleasure that turned into lasting grief.

But, *mira*, take a look, in Jesus, we get a glimpse of one of God's most beautiful characteristics. *Buenos notices!* It's called mercy. Jesus stood near the accused woman. Her dark eyes were filled with fright. And with stiff nerves, her soul was jammed with regret. She braced herself for the first stones. And while haughty Pharisees demanded that Jesus render a verdict, they gripped rocks in their own fists. They growled with vengeance.

Here is what came next: "Jesus bent down and started to write on the ground with his finger. When they kept questioning, he straightened up and said to them, 'Let any one of you who is without sin be the first to throw a stone at her'" (John 8:7, NIV). By the Pharisees' standards, maybe even by *our* standards, Jesus' reaction made no sense. *Por qué?* Why would he defend a sinner? *Amigas*, he does so because that's who he is. That's what he does. And that's why he came. He came to forgive us…so that we, too, can forgive. And through his forgiveness, our sin-filled lives have a second chance. Our relationships can mend, and our dark feelings toward those who hurt us can be transformed. That's the power of forgiveness.

But if you're the kind of *muchacha* who eats skepticism at every meal, Jesus takes one more step just for you. The adulterous woman's sin was plastered on neon signs all around the village. No one could miss it. But, Jesus transformed the scene. When those who wanted to punish her walked away, that *chica* must have heaved a sigh of relief bigger than the Red Sea.

Then Jesus turned and locked his compassionate eyes on hers, saying "Go and sin no more." Now, she might have been stunned at that simple instruction. And you'd better believe she left the market square, pinching herself to make sure what just happened was true. She might have tried to calm her drumming heart, knowing how close she came to being mush under rocks.

This man Jesus had the power to forgive, the love to set free, and the kindness to give new life. He taught forgiveness not only to her but also to the angry, rock-throwing crowd.

Ay Dios mio. Could some of us be among them? Digging deep, we have to admit it. Even today, we grip those stones in our manicured hands. And, with gritted teeth, we swing back, ready to hurl them...

> ...at the *esposo* who dared cheat on us.
> ...at those who abused us.
> ...at the relative who turned a back on us.
> ...at the jury that rendered an unfair decision.
> ...at the person who took our child's life.

And then, if we ourselves tumbled in the ditch of mistakes or wrong-doings, we grab an even larger stone. In the *silencio* of night, we use it to beat our own guilt-laden chest.

What Did Jesus Write?

And what about those accusers? Jesus took care of them too. He looked at them. He watched, waited, and gazed at each face. He saw each sin-stained heart. And he observed the rage that boiled among them. He didn't blame, confront, or call out to them in condemnation. He simply bent over and wrote on the dirt with his finger.

The Bible doesn't tell us what Jesus wrote in the dirt that day. But with a tad of audacity and tons of humility, this *muchacha* will dare to guess what Jesus wrote. It was a message for all of humanity, including you and me: *Soon I'll die to make you clean; then I'll rise to keep you loved, to show you how to forgive, and to set you free.*

If this truth is so simple to understand, why does bitterness and unforgiveness accompany millions at night? Because although we know Jesus' tender heart, we stick to our own notions:

Jesus says it's forgiven. But we still replay those hurtful images.

Jesus assures us he'll erase the pain. We dwell in our hurt.

Jesus urges us to forgive. We're stuck in the "what if it happens again?"

Jesus says vengeance is in his hands. We take it back in our own.

What's It All About?

The Word says that all things turn to good for those who love God. Remember how I questioned that promise when the verdict was read? God had the answer all along. But I didn't see that our complete, unconditional, and genuine forgiveness would be a turning, not just to "good" but to the best—the greatest and *más dulce*, sweetest aroma forgiveness can bring.

I hate to repeat, but *chicas*, this salsa we are called to dance is not about our own emotions of grief and rage and resentment. It's not about the person who wronged us. It's not about the pain we have. It's not about the brokenness we cradle. It's all about honoring God, obeying the commandment to forgive, and relishing in our new, fresh, and *free* lives.

I may be getting a bit personal with you, but let me suggest that God may be tapping at your heart. Without an ounce of impatience, the Lord is waiting to see what you'll choose. Will you harbor your right to bitterness? Or *en vez*, honor the divine right to request forgiveness?

Knowing we can choose the latter, *amigas*, we don't have to grit our teeth anymore. Instead, we can drop the condemning rocks and lose the extra weight of rancor. *No más*, no more harboring hostility. *No más* replaying hurtful images. *No más* planning victim pity-parties. *No más* nursing notions of vengeance. And *no más* running fingers over the ridge of old scars.

We close the door to the HELL department.

And sweeping out those toxic emotional cinders, with a clean soul, we take residency in God's peace. We put on the garment of freedom and set off on a new beginning. The serenity we thought we'd lost forever is restored, and I invite you, *chica*, take a look. Get closer to the reflection in the mirror. A younger you, a softer you, and a peaceful you stares back. Don't you just want to dance the salsa of freedom?

Go ahead because you're refreshed by the sweet fragrance of forgiveness. It's a different you, alive and free. Your smiling lips whisper, "*Señor* Jesus, *gracias. Que libertad,* what freedom you gave me." *Puedo respirar,* I can breathe, smile, sing, and rest at night because all is now well, truly well with my soul."

10

Who Invited Fear to My Fiesta?

Joy is the absence of fear.

"I don't believe in the Bible," a friend told me years ago. "It's full of contradictions."

Muchacha, I was shocked. What was her problem? Her comment bordered on that of a confirmed heretic. But as a novice Christian, I scratched my head, wondering how to respond. And through the years, as I dug through chapter after chapter and book after book, I wondered about some seeming contradictions too.

For example, in Ecclesiastes, we read we need to fear God, and then in the book of Psalm, we're instructed never to fear.

Confusion big time, right? Here's what clarified for me: My first fear is that my writing might not resonate with you, and that you will stop reading and not finish the book. I fear that you'll allow the fear factor to silence the salsa playing in your hearts. I fear that I will fail to communicate clearly how completely God has transformed my *vida loca* into *vida de amor*.

This kind of fear prompts me to try harder, to choose words and insights that will penetrate barriers so God may touch your very soul.

But, *caramba*, a second type of fear is also present in me. I fear I might get a terminal disease and never see this book in readers' hands. Or I'm afraid something might happen to *mi esposo*, *mis niños*, or grandchildren—and that the resulting grief would rob me of any trace of creativity.

Here's the thing: the first kind of fear nudges me to do my best. This second one threatens to paralyze me.

How simple it is to differentiate the two kinds of fear in Scripture: I'm afraid I won't please God, so my life's passion is to obey God's Word. That's a *bueno* kind of fear. On the other hand, the toxic, paralyzing and debilitating fear can't and shouldn't have a place in our Latina heart.

The Unknown

That's a simple insight. We understand it but still, fear accompanies us like our cell phones. It's always there and way too often, it rings to bring anxiety and panic. So, let's figure out the path to silence and defeat it.

First we'll analyze one more difference: a healthy kind of fear nudges us to correct what we know today. But the other kind of fear, with its unhealthy and destructive nature, urges us to worry about what might happen tomorrow. *Locura*! How crazy is that? We worry about something that hasn't happened. About something that isn't here yet. And about possibilities that may never exist.

Could it be that Jesus knew that? That's why in the Gospel of Matthew, he said, Stop worrying about silly stuff—what you'll eat or wear. I'll take care of you. *Mañana*'s troubles will take care of themselves.

But this *chica*, dancing to the world's beat, didn't listen. Instead, that fear for *mañana* flooded my nights with anxiety. Remember when I related my visit to the ophthalmologist? He sat me in a special chair and asked me to place my chin on a metal rest. And after he shone a tiny light into my eyes, he leaned back and frowned, giving me *malas noticias*. "There's nothing we can do."

Dios mio. Those words gripped me like iron claws. I was going blind.

The thought of becoming blind made me sick with fear. And what was the reason? The unknown. How would I live in total darkness? *No sé.* I didn't know. How would I perform the work of a mom and a wife? *No sé.* How *will* I navigate through life? *No sé.* Like Abuela's *queso empanadas, mañana*'s challenges stuffed my heart with fear.

I don't know! All the unknowns nearly turned my world upside down.

We all experience that when crisis pops like an intruder. What will we do should a situation reach its worst? For the moment, we're okay with what we see. You've been there, haven't you? We all have at one time or another. Maybe not facing permanent blindness, but with vision blurred by sad tears perhaps. We wonder what's next. We see the car in the driveway, but don't know what we'll do when the bank repossesses it. We earn a paycheck this week, but don't know how far it will go. We wonder how long we can endure the heartache in our relationships. We don't know how to cure the loneliness we bring to bed at night. Our health wanes, and we don't know if we'll heal. Will our kids be safe? We don't know. If the economy gets worse, how will we face that? We don't know. And the evening news generates more distress with details of violence and threats. *Cuando termina?* When will it end? We don't know that either.

Phew! *Amigas*, with all that, do you think the end times are here? You'd better believe it. We've reached *el fino*. It's time to *end* the cramping of our stomachs and the biting of our nails. And the only way to end our fear is to learn how we gave it power, where it came from, and learn to defeat it.

So They Lied to Us

Right about now you might be thinking of the junk that has piled up on your own life. And with a tad of skepticism, you're wondering how you can shake off that fear, that uncertainty, and that wacky worry. It's okay. You're not alone. If you would ask any *chica* to be *muy honesta*, really honest, she'll tell you there's definitely something she fears. The rich fear they'll lose their wealth. The successful folks fear their laurels will fade. The unemployed fear an empty pantry. The lonely fear empty nights. The overweight fear their diets won't work. And even the blind worry about what the next hurdle will be.

Un momentito. Wait a minute—did I say the blind worry? We do. But I have learned the secret to live a life with rich color, dimension, and sweet celebration. And since you and I have become close *amigas* as we turned the pages of this book together, I'm going to give you the formula. The pattern patented by God to show me that even after losing my sight, my son, and the other stuff I experienced in life, I could still find joy.

That's right, I had to find it. Maybe you do too. You have to learn to look for it. It's hidden in the midst of endless messages of the world that lie to us, telling us that we'll find it in the "happiness" masked by what we see, hear, and wish to experience.

The Secret

Did you know that God didn't create us to live a life of mere success, calmness, or prosperity? God created us for joy. That's right. We are meant to live a life that's rich with the fullness of joy.

This truth is something of a secret, hidden from most of us. Too many of us have fallen for the illusion that happiness is the goal for all people to pursue. But for God, our happiness is not enough. God wants us to savor a life with treasures that no one sees, yet everyone longs for. God created us to thrive, not just survive. To blaze a new trail, not follow a mundane rut. And while a salsa tune echoes in our head, the Spirit invites us to dance to the music of God's promises and to taste joy, delicious and real.

God's joy is no temporary high, but a conviction that penetrates emotional hurdles, that overrides circumstances and resonates in our hearts even when the day's bad news tries to muffle the music in our souls. God created us to delight in joy, to live it and let it fuel our every step, decision, and action.

A Recipe for Joy

Por favor, someone tell me how to get that joy. Here's how it works. To begin, we sift out the lie that events must dictate how we feel. If that were the case, this blind *muchacha* would be eating the *sopa de dolor*, the soup of sorrow.

Let me give you a detail of what happens from the time I get up. This is my morning routine. First, I get out of bed. And guess what. I can't see the way to the bathroom. Everything is dark gray. No light illuminates my way; no eyeglasses bring focus to my world. So the day starts with a challenge.

But here's what I do: before my feet hit the floor, my thoughts open the window of praises to God. Okay, you *muchachas* who might be rolling your eyes at this, stay with me. I realize I could be focused on what I lack. Dreading another day in darkness, consumed with self-pity, wondering how I'll make it from one room to the next, from one minute to the next. Instead I choose to praise God for that new day—because I consider the alternative.

No, I put my feet inside my slippers, and while my hair is still a mess and my arms stretch out so I don't run into walls, I dare claim joy. *Sí*, I claim joy for the day. True, trouble might show up. But *amigas,* joy has nothing to do with a trouble-free life. Joy has everything to do with the absence of fear.

Perhaps you don't open your eyes to physical darkness, but you wake up wondering if you still love the husband sleeping next to you, or worrying about the teenager who didn't come home until

3:00 a.m, or stifling the groans or tears of physical pain. Whatever circumstances inspire your fear, you feel the weight of the covers as if they are the weight of your burdens and you aren't sure if you can throw them off to face another day.

Where is joy to be found in that? *Queridas*, find peace and joy in this: All of your pain, all of your heartaches are already written in God's divine book. None of the ugly stuff that strikes discord in our lives escapes God's watchful eyes. They are listed in the chapter called "She'll go through this." So, you can be sure that God has also written the solution.

The Make-Over

God's happily-ever-after often requires us to start over with a new once-upon-a-time. *Sí*, a new beginning is mandatory. *Cómo?* Like a recipe that's turned out bad, we need to dump it in the trash and start over. If you want freedom from fear, you'll have to go through the soul make-over, too.

First, we stop that *loca* routine that says we're too busy to counsel with God. We leave behind those excuses—too much laundry, too many kid's activities, too many church activities, to much work to do. Sigh...no time for God.

But here's a piece of *buenas noticias*: God is still available for consultation, advice, and guidance. This is not to mistake the Lord of all as a servant. Rather, we approach God as Divine Ruler of our lives, the One who knows, perceives, and reveals the best path for us.

So, knowing that God is far wiser than we'll ever be, we settle in the seat of preparation. Then we wait. Yes, we sit still, *en silencio*, quiet and calm enough to let God's Word slip into our soul. This process comes before we make any decision, entertain any plan, or try to follow through with any recipe for success. We seek the Holy

Spirit's input first because, "If God doesn't build the house, the builders only build shacks. If God doesn't guard the city, the night watchman might as well nap. It's useless to rise early and go to bed late, and work your worried fingers to the bone. Don't you know he enjoys giving rest to those he loves?" (Psalm 127:1-3, THE MESSAGE).

God does the building. God calls the shots. God equips us for the journey. And then, we can expect excellence with no regrets. And *que bueno*. To you and me whom God loves, the Spirit provides for every detail—a full night's sleep, a serene soul, and a mind free from anxious thoughts.

So, if you're serious about starting over, *chica*, make an appointment with the Divine Planner, the All-knowing Architect and All-powerful Consultant. Let God take the lead. Let the Lord bring on the next opportunity. And humming your favorite salsa, you'll watch how God brings the glorious outcome, sealed with joy.

Wise (and Not Stupid) Women

Amigas, you might not like this next step, but here we go. Before we get into the details, let's stuff our sensitivity in the junk drawer, and wearing the cologne of courage, face the truth. If we want to achieve all of the above, we need to correct our false images of *Dios*. And if, in a moment of insanity, we've refused correction, then we can't do that anymore because "whoever hates correction is stupid" (Proverbs 12:1b).

Estúpido? Did we read that right? How could God's Word include such a rude word? Well, *chicas*, the sad truth is that it fits us. Or, maybe I shouldn't include you, but I'll be the first to wave my hand in the air and say, "That was me...in more ways than one." Before my life centered on Jesus, I was one foolish, fear-filled, joyless *chica*. And contrary to what you might think, being stupid isn't the opposite of being intelligent. Instead, stupidity comes from

133

distorting what is correct and true, or putting our own interpretation to what God clearly instructs.

"Stupid" doesn't fit us. Rather, without pride, we accept that intelligence ricochets underneath that dark hair of ours—intelligence enough to understand that if God created us for joy, God also gave us the map to achieve the goal. Who better to trust with our joy-filled future that the One who is the same yesterday, today, and forever, the One who knows the future? You see, if we don't belong in the stupid group, then we belong to the *familia* of corrected, wise, and confident *hijas*, daughters of the King.

We Simply Forgot

If this recipe for joy is so simple, why isn't it simmering in the kitchens of *chicas* all over the planet? Because we were raised to steep the *té* of worry. We learned this from our teachers, from our *mamis*, our *tias*, and our *abuelas*. That's right. They taught us to worry. And as we learned, we tasted the bitter dregs of fear.

But *está bien*, it's okay. We can change this and exchange that bitter *té* for something light and sweet. Here's how God did it for me.

A few years ago, my oldest son and his wife were praying for a way to get health insurance. My son had been laid off and his insurance coverage ran out. To make things a bit tougher, they were expecting our second grandchild. "*Dios mio! Ayúdalos*, help them, *por favor*," was my fervent prayer. Being the concerned *mami*, I wanted to fix their problem, to make it all better. Unable to do so, I fought worry and had to spray mace on the fear that attacked me.

But *amigas*, here was my lesson: My two-year-old granddaughter played, giggled, said cute things, and hopped around without a care in the world. Oh, *niña preciosa*, I thought, if you only knew what trouble your *mami* and *papi* are in.

Then, God tapped my soul. "C'mon, *muchacha*, don't you remember?" the Holy Spirit seemed to say. "Jesus called a little child to stand among them, and he said: 'I tell you the truth, unless you change and become like little children, you will never enter the kingdom of heaven'" (see Matthew 18:1-3).

Become like a little child? I needed to learn that. So I observed my two year-old hum a nursery rhyme. No worries. No anxious thinking. No nervous stomach. In her innocence, she trusted, simply trusted, while I was letting fear eat me for lunch.

And *que pasó?* As always, God answered our prayers, timely and clearly. The Lord made health insurance available at the precise moment it was most needed. We cheered with gratitude, but I considered how different those months of waiting would have been if we had imitated that two-year-old child and simply played and trusted.

That's why Jesus said, "I tell you the truth." Has he ever told us anything but the truth? *Cielos,* heavens no. But he emphasized it in that Scripture, as if to say, "I'm not kidding. Unless you change and become worry-free, trustful, confident, and free, you'll never see heavenly joy, on earth or on the other side of eternity."

So what's left? *Nada* but to go back to the time we were *niñas.* Back to the time when we trusted, simply trusted in those who loved us. Only when our thinking, our attitudes, our emotions and longings return to that place of innocent trust in God, in our heavenly *Papi,* only then will joy explode within us.

Let's Get Practical

Maybe this insight has found a comfortable place in your heart. But in the reality of life, the peace and joy of childlike trust may not stay there, not for long. It might fizzle out before you get your next cup of *café con leche.* You like what you are reading, but you need to close the book. You have to close it quickly because the *niños* want a drink or *tu esposo* wants to talk. Or perhaps the phone rings and an *amiga* accepts your invitation for dinner *con la familia*—and that reminds you the house needs to be cleaned, badly. And after the interruption, you discover that the burden that was nagging at you last night is still there.

All these real issues of life make God's invitation to find joy in your life vanish like soap bubbles in dirty dishwater.

As we age, the years do seem to accumulate like dirty dishes in that sink of murky dishwater. Before we know it, the kitchen of our lives just doesn't look good. But I have learned that each year brings reason to celebrate. I could have been gone last year, but I'm still here. *Chicas*, bring out the flan and the sweet fruit punch, and don't worry about the dishes. I'm celebrating each month and rejoicing with each year of life.

But as years turn like pages in a book, there is something we try to ignore, a fact that we tend to forget. This forgetfulness is not only found in older *chicas*. Young *muchachas* who are still dancing 'til dawn, you forget too. We forget what God has done for us.

This has been a problem since biblical times. When God told the courageous leader Joshua to take the sometimes-ungrateful Israelites across the Jordan River, the Lord had to give one more instruction. "Take some rocks, Josh," God told his man. "Take rocks across the river with you, and pile them up on the other side. Then, the generations that come after you will see the rock pile and you'll have a reason to remember how I parted the river so you could cross over into the land of promises."

Queridas amigas, who could forget such an amazing miracle? But God knew that the Israelites, being human, would certainly forget. *Sí*. They would forget. And so do we. And so, God gave them reminders. And we need the same.

The Scriptures are a kind of rock pile, a tangible reminder that jars the memory of God's people—to remember that God is capable of doing the impossible.

We also have the Rock called Jesus. He's the one who, through the Holy Spirit, will whisper to us at night—Do not fear. I have done impossible things. I raised the dead. I healed thousands. I've taken wayward children and returned them to the fold.

When we remember all this, we can't settle for fleeting happiness, superficial success, or fragile financial security. Not us. With vibrant, Latina passion, we can embrace the joy that conquers fear, that defeats its effects and sings victory at every stage.

Living la Vida de Amor

To dance into a brighter, joy-filled future, we need to recognize the fears, mistakes, and missteps we have taken. Remember when we trusted God only in good times but not in bad? We accepted the blessings but cursed the burdens. We only wanted to hear biblical words of comfort, not prophetic words of conviction. We might have consented to attend worship on Sunday, but dashed to the *vida loca* Monday through Saturday. And, in *un momento* of foolish deception, we assumed God would accept such half-hearted commitment.

No más. No more. We're driving forward now and no more glancing into the rearview mirror of life. We, new Latinas with a sizzling passion to find joy. To live *la vida de amor*, of confidence and significance, we are tossing misconceptions out the window. We're declaring freedom from fear. We're shouting to the world, "We're different!" We may live a life jammed with troubles, but we thrive in a life that's replete with joy. Not because we're ignoring reality, but because we're identifying who's in control. We've formed a bond, deep and eternal with the One who has the answers for problems bigger than life. God is greater than our pain and more powerful than our problems.

Take the last sip of your *café con leche, muchacha*. Then put the cup down, along with the old fear-filled you. And with a new smile of confidence, lean in and listen to the promise for joy. God is calling your name: "Do not fear, for I have redeemed you. I have summoned you by name; you are mine. When you pass through the waters, I will be with you; and when you pass through the rivers, they will not sweep over you. When you walk through the fire, you will not be burned; the flames will not set you ablaze. For I am the LORD, your God..." (Isaiah 43:1-3).

Claro que sí, of course, reassurance and joy will filter through. The waters of trouble will exist. The fire of pain will surround us. But God will not be far above or a great distance away. The Spirit will be right here with us, assuring us that no one and nothing can ever separate us from God's loving presence. And this is what puts fear in its grave, once and for all. It's the reassurance that joy is ours. It's the determination that greets us in the morning. The peace that accompanies us through each day. And the assurance that, even when we face *malas noticias*, we have nothing to fear.

Something to Celebrate

Women back in biblical times wore robes. Today, we wear jeans. They lived in tents; we live in condos. But inside, we're the same. At one time or another, we have all tasted the bitterness of life and we have also savored triumph. Miriam was one of us. When she was in the middle of the crowd when the Egyptians chased her people, she witnessed God's miracle and what she saw banished her fear. And she didn't just sit at home, smiling as she rolled out her *tortillas*. No, *señora*. She gathered musical instruments, "and all the women followed her with tambourines, dancing. Miriam led them in singing, 'Sing to God—what a victory!'" (Exodus 15:20-21, THE MESSAGE).

That's one passionate, smart *mujer*. She celebrated the same victory that you and I already have. She probably had a little Latina blood in her because she danced, *amigas*. She threw a fiesta to celebrate God's mighty power that parted the Red Sea. That same God will part our sea of troubles too. And while we wait, we prepare our heart with joy.

While all other *chicas* are fretting about unanswered problems, we're confident God is already preparing the solutions. Others are tossing awake at night. We rest in the soft pillow of peace. Others are adding wrinkles to their faces; we are shaking out our garments of joy. Others hunger for happiness, we delight in joy. We know the kind of life others miss. And we live the life others would die for.

Too many *chicas* are lost in the complicated tango of tension and anxiety. But you and I, *amigas*, sway to the simplicity of God's salsa, dancing without hesitation, without doubt, and without fear at a divine fiesta. But, sorry, *lo siento*. This elite reception is by invitation only. Surely by now you should have received yours, because you are among those created for joy.

So, *vamos*. Get on your feet. Can you feel the contagious, rhythmic beat? The sweet melody of joy is playing just for you, the new you—free and confident. So, lift up your chin and give a passionate, sassy twirl. *Let's salsa!*

Glossary

abrazo — hug
abuela — grandmother
adentro — inside
adiós — goodbye
agua — water
amiga; amigas — friend; friends (fem.)
aun más — still more
ayúdalos — help them

bueno — good
buenas notices — good news
buñuelo — fritter made with flour and eggs, fried in oil;
doughnut; dumpling; (colloq.) may also refer to anything
done poorly; a failure

café con leche — coffee with milk
caramba — an interjection, usually in surprise or frustration;
e.g., jeez; cripes; darn
casi siempre — almost always
chica / chicas — girl(s); affectionate term for women
Cristo — Christ
chuño — dried potatoes, used for making soup
cielos — skies
claro — of course; sure
cómo? — how
completamente — completely

con — with
créeme — believe me
creo — I believe; I think
cuando — when

día y noche — day and night
días — days
diferente — different
difícil — difficult
Dios — God
Dios mio — my God

el nos perdonó — he forgave us
empanadas — meat pies made of pastry
en vez — instead
escucha — listen
espera un momentito — wait a minute
esperanza — hope and expectation
esposo — husband
está bien — it's fine
estúpido — stupid

familia — family
flores — flowers

grande — large
gringa — American; Yankee (usually Anglo; fem.)

hasta cuando — how long?
helados de chocolate — chocolate ice cream
hijita — little one
honesto — honest; truthful
horas — hours

importante — important
incorrecto — wrong; also rude

libertad — freedeom; liberty

malas noticias — bad news
mañana — tomorrow
mariachi — musical genre that originated in Western Mexico
  and that is particularly distinctive for its integration of string
  instruments, featuring the Mexican **guitarrón** and **vihuela**
  but also including the guitar, violin, and occasionally a harp,
  as well as percussion and brass such as the trumpet
más dulce — sweeter
mi esposo — my husband
momento (un momento) — one moment
muchacha — young woman (informal)
mujeres — women
muy — very

niña / niño — little girl / little boy
no hay duda — no doubt
no más — no more
número uno — number one

pollo con arroz — chicken with rice
pon atencion — pay attention
por favor — please
por qué? — why?
por qué no? — why not?
por seguro — for certain
problema — problem
pronto — soon
puedo respirar — I can breathe

qué? — what?

que bueno — how good; how wonderful

qué pasa? — what's happening? what's up?

qué pasó? — what happened?

que pena — how sad

qué tiene de malo — what is wrong?

querida — darling; dear friend

queso — cheese

salsa — sauce (lit.); also a group of musical styles from Cuba and the dance forms that correspond to such music

señor / señora — sir / madam; Mr. / Mrs.; gentleman / lady

Señor, el — the Lord (God)

sí — yes

sigo esperando — still waiting

silencio — silence

sopa de pollo — chicken soup

sutilmente — subtly

termina — end; conclude; finish

todo — everything; the whole or entirety

toda una vida — a lifetime

tres — three

una noche — one night

vamos — let's go

vida de amor — life of love

vida loca — crazy life

y tú? — and you?

yo no sé — I don't know

If You Enjoyed *Simply Salsa*
You'll Also Love These Candid and Conversational Books from Faithful and Inspiring Women!

The Flavor of Our Hispanic Faith
Karen Valentin with Edwin Aymat

Karen's stories bring to the life the sacred and secular, making them one and the same. She reminds us that God is in the rice and beans that we eat and in the songs that we sing. God is present in the simple acts of love, friendship, and faith that Hispanics share at home, church, and in the community. I was moved by the power of her faith in the vignettes and blessed by the prayers."

   —Pablo R. Diaz, Vice President of Ministries, *Guideposts*

"Christian readers, whether of Hispanic heritage or not, will find inspiration in the fifty-six stories in this small but moving book."

Also available i

978-0-8170-15

I'm a Piece of W

"I'm most impr
insecurities, mis
biblical scriptures, this book offers practical advice on how to see yourself through God's eyes, to embrace his vision of the real you, celebrate your uniqueness, forgive yourself, renew, forgive others, dream, and pursue perfection. What a joy and how encouraging it was to read this book!"

 —Venus Bivens (as reviewed on Amazon.com) 978-0-8170-1571-8 $16.00

What Eve Didn't Tell Us: Sex, Casseroles, and a Life of Faith
Sue Thomen Dolquist and Jane M. Wood

"What I most appreciated about this book was its honesty and how it made me laugh."

   —Leah Jenson (as reviewed on Amazon.com)

This humorous, yet compelling first-person look into the lives of two women explores the complexities of continually balancing marriage, work, parenting, and self in ways that our mothers and grandmothers could not have imagined. 978-0-8170-1416-2 $12.00

To order Judson Press resources, call 800-458-3766
or visit www.judsonpress.com.

JUDSON PRESS
PUBLISHERS SINCE 1824